Strategic Marketing for the Digital Age

Strategic Marketing for the Digital Age

Grow Your Business With Online and Digital Technology

BILL BISHOP

HarperBusiness
HarperCollins*PublishersLtd*

STRATEGIC MARKETING FOR THE DIGITAL AGE:
GROW YOUR BUSINESS WITH ONLINE AND DIGITAL TECHNOLOGY

http://www.harpercanada.com

HarperCollins books may be purchased for educational, business, or sales promotional use. For information please write: Special Markets Department, HarperCollins Canada, 55 Avenue Road, Suite 2900, Toronto, Ontario, Canada M5R 3L2.

Canadian Cataloguing in Publication Data

Bishop, Bill, 1957–
Strategic marketing for the digital age –
grow your business with online and digital technology.

Includes bibliographical references.
ISBN 0-00-255433-X (bound)
ISBN 0-00-638637-7 (pbk)

1. Marketing – Data processing. 2. Database marketing. 3. Teleshopping.
4. Internet marketing. 5. Marketing – Technological innovations. I. Title.

HF5415.1265.B57 1996 658.8'00285 C96-930733-0

---

99 00 01 02 03 04 ❖ HC 6 5 4 3 2 1

Printed and bound in the United States

To my son Douglas

A 21st Century Digital Boy

CONTENTS

Acknowledgments xiii
Preface: Digital Marketing — Like Science Fiction Come to Life xv

SECTION ONE:
AN INTRODUCTION TO DIGITAL MARKETING 1

CHAPTER 1: THE PIONEERS OF DIGITAL MARKETING 3
- *Finding the Perfect Refrigerator* 4
- *Car Care in Cyberspace* 6
- *Your Virtual Home Office* 6
- *The Fast-Paced Digital Economy* 7
- *Staggering Array of Choices* 8
- *More Than Just the Internet* 8
- *Marketing Technopia* 9
- *Overview of Chapters* 11

CHAPTER 2: THE DIGITAL MARKETING ENVIRONMENT 13
- *Changes in the Marketing World* 14
- *What Makes Digital Marketing Different* 15
- *The Customer Is the Focus* 17
- *Develop Capabilities, Not Products* 19
- *Change Channels and Be Different* 19
- *Choose from All the Digital Marketing Tools* 20
- *The Changing Role of Traditional Media* 21
- *Provide Quality Content or Something Useful* 23
- *What You Need to Do* 26

CHAPTER 3: THE STRATEGIC DIGITAL MARKETING MODEL 30
- *Start with a Strategy* 31
- *The Foundation of Your Empire* 31
- *Your Digital Domain* 34
- *Digital Marketing in Action* 42
- *The Beginning of Your Empire* 50

CHAPTER 4: THE POWER OF DIGITAL TECHNOLOGY 51
- *The Basics of Bits and Bytes* 52
- *The Basics of the Personal Computer* 53
- *Modems and Bandwidth* 57
- *Software You Need to Understand* 58
- *The Basics of Online Technology* 59
- *The Many Faces of the Internet* 62
- *Computer Bulletin Board Services (BBS)* 64
- *The Battle For Bandwidth* 65
- *The Multimedia Revolution* 66
- *Get Acquainted with the Digital World* 67

SECTION TWO:

PLANNING YOUR DIGITAL MARKETING STRATEGY 69

CHAPTER 5: CREATE YOUR DIGITAL VISION 71
- *Long-Term Digital Goals* 72
- *Medium-Term Digital Goals* 75
- *Short-Term Digital Goals* 79
- *Hold a Digital Strategy Session* 86

CHAPTER 6: RESEARCH YOUR DIGITAL MARKET 87
- *The Digital Demographics* 88
- *The Digital Communications Audit* 91
- *The Popularity of Digital Devices* 95

CHAPTER 7: START YOUR CUSTOMER DATABASE 98
- *How Databases Work* 99
- *Why You Need a Customer Database* 102
- *Benefits You Will Realize from a Customer Database* 105
- *How to Set Up Your Customer Database* 108
- *Attract More Customers and Have Better Relationships* 111

CHAPTER 8: CHOOSE YOUR DIGITAL TOOLS 112
- *The Telephone: Everyone Uses One* 113
  - *Voice Mail*
  - *Voice Mail Broadcast*
  - *A 1-900 Number*
  - *Reverse 1-900*
  - *Pay Phone Services*
  - *Prepaid Long-Distance Calling Cards*
  - *Cellular Telephones*
- *Digital Cards and Coupons* 121
  - *Loyalty Club Cards*
  - *Digital Coupons*
  - *Digital Cheques*
- *Online Tools: Not Just the Web* 124
  - *The Internet*
    - *Mighty E-Mail*
    - *Mail List Servers*
    - *The World Wide Web*
    - *Search Engines*
    - *Links from Popular Sites*
    - *Strategic Web Partners*
    - *Online Shopping*
    - *Newsgroups*
    - *File Transfer Protocol (FTP) Sites*
  - *Bulletin Board Services (BBS)*
    - *Choosing Between BBS and Web*
    - *Get the Ball Rolling*
  - *Commercial Online Services*
  - *Proprietary Internet Platforms*
  - *Cable Networks*
  - *In-store kiosks*
- *Multimedia Tools* 141
  - *CD-ROM*
  - *CD-ROM and Online Services*
  - *Floppy Disks*
  - *Video Game Cartridges*
- *Fax Tools* 143
  - *Fax Broadcast*
  - *Fax-On-Demand*
  - *Fax Mailboxes*

• *Other Digital Tools* 144
Proprietary Software
Electronic Forms
Pagers
Virtual Reality Arcade Machines
• *Coming Soon* 146
Digital Videodisk (DVD)
Wireless Personal Digital Assistants (PDA)
Interactive Television
Video-Mail
Vitual Reality Online

CHAPTER 9: DREAM UP YOUR DIGITAL PROMOTION 149
• *Digital Roadside Attractions* 150
• *Proactive Digital Programs* 160
• *Direct Digital Sales Programs* 163
• *Put It All Together* 165

CHAPTER 10: PUT ALL THE BITS AND BYTES TOGETHER 166
• *The Information Provider: Big Bob's Hardware Emporium* 167
• *The Database Marketer: The Gourmet Baby Food Company* 168
• *The Proactive Integrator: Webbed Feet Film and Printing* 170
• *The Digital Community: International Association of Sperm Bank Operators* 171
• *The Smart Innovator: The Bowling Ball Alarm Agency* 173
• *The Interactive Undertaker: Frederick's Funeral Homes* 174
• *The Digital Communicator: Liability & Lawsuits* 175
• *The Strategic Digital Bartender: Bernie's Bar & Grill* 176
• *Requiem for Traditional Marketing* 178

CHAPTER 11: BUILD YOUR DIGITAL COMMAND CENTER 179
• *Integration in the Digital Economy* 180
• *Get Online!* 182
• *Setting Up a Web Site* 183
• *A Network-Wide Internet Connection* 184
• *Install a Bulletin Board System (BBS)* 185
• *Other Digital Capabilities* 186
• *Connecting to Your Database* 187
• *A Future Migration Path* 187
• *Ready to Rock 'n' Roll* 188

SECTION THREE:
RUNNING YOUR DIGITAL MARKETING PROGRAM 189

CHAPTER 12: LAUNCH YOUR DIGITAL MARKETING PROGRAM 191
- *The Launch* 192
- *The Ongoing Process* 197
- *The Expansion of Your Program* 198

CHAPTER 13: ASSESS YOUR DIGITAL SUCCESS 200
- *Hits, Hits, Hits* 201
- *Invalid Assessment Tools* 203
- *The Problem of Disk Caching* 203
- *Assessing Web Display Advertising* 204
- *Measuring Quality and Contact* 204
- *Measuring Other Digital Tools* 205
- *Database Tracking* 205

SECTION FOUR:
THE ETHICS OF DIGITAL MARKETING 207

CHAPTER 14: PROTECTING CUSTOMER PRIVACY 209
- *The Potential for Abuse* 210
- *Safeguard the Bond of Trust* 212
- *Open Communication — Key to Ethical Digital Marketing* 214
- *Ownership of Personal Data* 215
- *Sensitivity to the Need for Privacy* 217

CHAPTER 15: PROTECTING YOUR DIGITAL RIGHTS 218
- *Domain Name Dilemma* 219
- *The Impossible Task of Digital Enforcement* 220
- *Digital Legal Liabilities* 222
- *Keeping Secrets in the Digital Age* 225
- *Electronic Money and Online Transactions* 227
- *Take the Digital High Road* 229

SECTION FIVE:
THE FUTURE OF DIGITAL MARKETING 231

CHAPTER 16: BEYOND TECHNOPIA 233
- *The Digital Boom Years (Year 2020)* 233
- *The Dawn of the Biological Economy (2096)* 235
- *The Year of the Joy Dimension (2525)* 236

Glossary of Terms 239
Suggested Reading 251

ACKNOWLEDGMENTS

As an independent businessperson, I've never been a natural team player. My instinct is to go it alone and do it myself. But writing this book has taught me the importance of getting help from talented friends and business associates. Luckily I have many of both and I can never hope to repay them for the time they spent, or the encouragement they provided. Regardless, I want to thank:

- Don Loney, my editor, who championed the book and gave freely of his vast experience and wisdom;
- Ginny McFarlane, who spent many hours proofreading each chapter, and gave me the benefit of her perspicacity and astute intellect;
- Curtis Verstraete, my business partner, who contributed his wide knowledge of marketing and digital technology, and provided sound words of advice whenever my imagination went too far;
- Lynne Shuttleworth and Andy Parks who helped with the editing and graphic design, and kept my business running smoothly while I was sequestered away working on the book;
- my mother and father, who gave me support when I needed it; and
- my five-year-old son Douglas, who played quietly while I wrote this book about "fidgital marketing."

I also want to express my gratitude to the following people who helped me with this book and supported the development of Bishop

Information Group Inc.: Carol Bonnett, Simone Lee, Diana Bishop, Elaine Bishop, John Narvali, Jorma Ikavalko, Peter Creaghan, Sara Creaghan, Dan Sullivan, Steve Barrett, John Shenstone, Kevin Nullmeyer, Sandra Matheson, Judith Tropianskaia, Susan Johnson, Ron Hansell, Malcolm Silver, John Lyons, Tim Falconer, Lynda Douglas, David Bowen, Doug Biggar, Kirk Biggar, Erik Berger, and Carmen Jarzabek.

My digital associates: I also want to thank my Macintosh Performa 5200CD computer, which never crashed or corrupted any of my files; my FirstClass™ BBS system, which kept the digital files moving fast and furious; InfoRamp, my Internet provider, for giving me enough bandwidth to surf the Web until all hours of the night, my SupraFax modem, for keeping the bits and bytes flowing; and my Microsoft Works software program, which will always be my favorite application.

PREFACE

DIGITAL MARKETING — LIKE SCIENCE FICTION COME TO LIFE

My interest in digital and online technology began when I fell in love with science fiction at about ten years of age. I read hundreds of great books by writers such as Robert Heinlein, Kurt Vonnegut Jr., and Isaac Asimov. I loved the fantastic tales set on far-off planets running wild with robots and aliens. I was especially intrigued by the incredible technology which made space travel and time travel possible. I couldn't wait for the future.

So when I got a part-time job working with computers in 1978, I was thrilled. Working on a massive mainframe computer, I felt like I was at the helm of a starship. Computers seemed to me like science fiction come to life. It was only a matter of time, I thought, before you and I would be living on Mars and traveling through time.

Of course, the future isn't what it used to be. Instead of blasting into hyperspace, computers have taken us into cyberspace. And instead of using computer technology to visit Neptune, we're using it to sell mutual funds and beer. But it's still exciting. And that's why digital marketing is interesting — it's a mind-boggling science fiction story come to life.

How else can you explain all the hype surrounding the Internet? Despite all its promise, few people can honestly claim they have made money by marketing on the Internet. And yet people still flock to it. Why? Because it's such incredible technology. Surfing the Internet, you're instantly seized by a sense of power. You can go anywhere in the world at the click of the mouse.

Digital marketing can be a fantastic voyage full of amazing gizmos and gadgets. Of course any voyage can also be fraught with hair-raising adventures and the odd evil villain. As you begin your journey, you may feel some trepidation. There is a danger digital technology will further erode our personal privacy, or cause us to lose touch with each other. These issues must be addressed or consumers will shun our attempts to use digital technology to sell our wares.

I hope you enjoy reading *Strategic Marketing for the Digital Age* and that you can use it to bring to life your own exciting science fiction story.

Bill Bishop
September 1996

SECTION ONE

AN INTRODUCTION TO DIGITAL MARKETING

CHAPTER 1

THE PIONEERS OF DIGITAL MARKETING

Valentine Michael Smith swam through the murky water for the deepest part of the pool. He (also) elected to stretch his time sense until seconds flowed past like hours, as he had much to contemplate. Smith still felt that he had "grokked" rightly the human word "God" — the confusion had come in his own failure in selecting the human words.

Stranger In A Strange Land
Robert A. Heinlein, 1961

In his wonderful book, *Stranger In A Strange Land*, Robert Heinlein tells the tale of Michael Valentine Smith, a human born and raised on Mars who returns to Earth as an adult. With little knowledge of humanity, Smith experiences culture shock and has a difficult time adapting to his new life on Planet Earth.

When it comes to digital marketing, each of us is also a "stranger in a strange land." The technology is so new that anyone who uses it is a pioneer. When you use digital tools, such as the Internet, to promote your business, there is little research or previous experience to guide you. Until now, the only way to learn what works best was to plunge into the water and see what happens.

Like Smith, we're also experiencing culture shock. Everywhere we turn, we're confronted with a whole new spectrum of technical words and phrases. Terms such as World Wide Web, online ordering, bulletin board services, electronic commerce, and e-mail marketing are being thrown around with increasing frequency by marketing consultants, academics, bureaucrats, media pundits, and just about everyone else involved in marketing products and services.

But what do all of these terms mean? How do these digital tools impact on the world of marketing, and how will they in the future? To provide answers to these questions is the reason I wrote this book. It's an attempt to bring some order to the field of digital marketing and to propose standard principles and models to help you develop your own digital marketing strategy. I look at all the digital tools available, not just the Internet, to help you put together a strategy which makes the most sense for your company, your products, your services, and, most importantly, your customers.

Perhaps the best way to start is to look ahead to the near future. After all, just about everyone involved in digital marketing admits the real benefits of this new technology will not be realized for a few years yet. So let's take a look — with a certain allowance for creative license — at what the world of marketing might be like in the year 2005.

FINDING THE PERFECT REFRIGERATOR

You need a new refrigerator. Your old one conked out last week and you have been ordering in pizza and chicken wings every night. But you don't have time to traipse across town visiting one appliance showroom after another. So you sit down at your computer to see if you can find a new refrigerator in cyberspace.

Through high-speed cable modem (a thousand times faster than the modems used way back in 1996), you log into the local cybermarket and enter "refrigerators" in the enquiry field. Instantly, you're presented with a long list of possible appliance dealers and manufacturers. You choose Marvelous Marvin's Freezer Emporium because it has a flashing bulletin promising you can win a *Trip Around the World*, just by visiting their interactive Build-Your-Own-Fridge Web site.

With a click of your mouse, you're greeted by an animated version of Marvelous Marvin who asks what type of refrigerator you're looking for. You explain (all Internet sites are now equipped with voice-response technology) that you're looking for one of those new refrigerators monitored through the Internet. Marvelous Marvin smiles and beckons you through an on-screen door to show you their latest model: The Internet-Fridge 5000.

You click your way in and around the 3-D refrigerator, checking its many high-tech features. You print out full-color pictures of the refrigerator on your laser printer, download the digital product video, and enter the *Trip Around the World* contest by leaving your video-mail address.

After searching through five other refrigerator sites, you decide to make your purchase from Marvelous Marvin, so you return to the site. Marvin greets you upon your return and now addresses you by name. You tell him you want to place an order. In the top left corner of your screen, you're greeted by a live video picture of a Marvelous Marvin sales representative.

You place your order and use your keyboard to send a deposit from your virtual bank account by encrypted e-mail. You click on the top right corner of your screen to access another live video of the plant manager, who thanks you for your order and then shows you — by a handheld camera — your refrigerator coming down the line. The whole process of shopping for your refrigerator takes less than an hour and you receive the lowest price offered by all major appliance dealers.

Two days later your refrigerator arrives by truck directly from the plant. The installer connects the unit to your house-wide Internet cable to monitor and correct any malfunctions, and also remotely control the level of energy use. A week later you get a video-mail message from Marvelous Marvin thanking you for your purchase, and asking if you would like to receive regular video-mail messages about special discounts for valued customers. You agree to the idea. Unfortunately, you don't win the Trip Around the World contest but your refrigerator works perfectly for many years.

CAR CARE IN CYBERSPACE

You're the marketing director of SpeedyCoil, a worldwide chain of 5,500 electric car maintenance franchises. You develop a digital marketing program to generate more repeat business at your outlets. You begin by setting up a Car Care Reminder Service in which each outlet gathers customer names and video-mail addresses (which in 2005 are as common as e-mail addresses were in 1998). When a customer comes into the outlet for battery maintenance and contact cleaning, information about the servicing is entered in a computer terminal linked to a central database. Three months later, the database sends a video-mail message to the customer, reminding him that his car needs to be serviced again. The video-mail also contains an electronic coupon.

When in place, this worldwide system is sending out more than 25,000 video-mail messages a day at virtually no transmission cost. Sales at each franchise grow an average of 25 percent as customers increase their use of your services on a regular basis. As well, your marketing costs drop 35 percent because expensive mass-media advertising is no longer necessary.

YOUR VIRTUAL HOME OFFICE

As a consultant in human resources, you work from your home office. You have no staff, but you have an electronic network of colleagues around the world. You want to expand your business by promoting your services using digital marketing.

You begin by establishing a World Wide Web site which includes a comprehensive directory listing the addresses of hundreds of human resources–related Web sites. You promote the presence of your Web site by placing a small ad in business and trade magazines, both print and online versions. In addition to your Web directory, you create a software program to help human resources departments generate statistical reports charting the relationship between safety awareness programs and worker compensation costs. The software program — called HRCalc — is available as a shareware program, and can be downloaded from your Web site.

You also use your Web site to gather the video-mail addresses of more than 15,000 human resources professionals across North America. You send them, in the blink of an eye, a regular video bulletin about human resources issues. Each video-mail newsletter contains digital video clips, full-color electronic brochures, and shareware programs. Because all the information you provide is useful and not completely self-serving, you gain a tremendous level of exposure in your industry, and turn the exposure into an ever-growing stable of quality clients.

THE FAST-PACED DIGITAL ECONOMY

Marketing programs like these will be possible in the near future. Many of them are possible today. In fact, these projected scenarios are probably conservative. In the year 2005, computers will be 20 times more powerful than today's models, and will be connected directly to the Internet (or another more advanced version of the Internet) through coaxial or fiber-optic cable. Sending and receiving video from your computer will be commonplace, as will video-conferencing. Software programs will be easy to build and adapt for your own use. Video-mail and e-mail will be more common than regular telephone calls. We will be carrying around handheld PDAs (Personal Digital Assistants) used to send and receive video images, and to access a universe of useful — and useless — information.

In this world of digital gadgetry, a new fast-paced digital economy will emerge. There will be companies that exist only inside computer networks. They will help people navigate through the maze of data and help them market their services there. Most business transactions will be made electronically, directly from the producer to the consumer, bypassing wholesalers and retailers. Every day, new opportunities for business will emerge as new technology is introduced and digital entrepreneurs test new ideas.

If you think these ideas are far-fetched, watch out. Remember, the Internet wasn't even mentioned in the mass media until the end of 1994. Now it's a household word.

STAGGERING ARRAY OF CHOICES

If you're involved in business, you'll be faced with a staggering array of choices in the next few years. You'll be called upon to take advantage of digital technology while not losing sight of your most important asset — your customers. Unfortunately, old models of marketing do not apply to the digital world. The models established for traditional mass marketing do not hold up in the digital marketing environment. An entirely new marketing model is required — a Strategic Digital Marketing Model.

MORE THAN JUST THE INTERNET

The growing popularity of the Internet, and the massive media hype surrounding its commercial potential, have triggered an avalanche of interest in using this new tool for marketing. All you have to do, the reasoning goes, is place your ad on the World Wide Web (the popular graphical platform of the Internet) and the world will beat an electronic path to your door. Well, I've been involved in marketing and online technology for more than 17 years, and I tell you it isn't that simple.

The profound impact of digital technology on the marketing environment involves much more than just the Internet. To view the

Internet as a marketing wonder drug is like thinking one vitamin a day will solve all your health problems. Of course, the Internet is an exciting medium (and I thoroughly examine its marketing potential in this book), but strategic digital marketing must look at all the other digital tools such as CD-ROMS, databases, digital video, e-mail, fax-on-demand systems, smart cards, 1-900 numbers, computer bulletin board systems (BBS) and the myriad of other digital tools which will emerge in the years to come.

A digital marketing strategy must also address how you combine these tools to achieve your business objectives. Ask yourself: "What do my customers want? What digital tools do they want to use? How will digital technology help me generate more sales and achieve my business goals." After asking these questions and looking at the whole picture, you'll realize there is more to this game than just the Internet.

So if you've become interested in digital marketing because of the Internet, this book challenges you to look much deeper into the issue. Think about how you can use all the digital tools rather than focusing just on the Internet. I call this process Strategic Digital Marketing because it brings together all of the digital tools and processes into a long-term strategic plan for your company or organization.

MARKETING TECHNOPIA

Strategic Digital Marketing also serves as a warning — a warning against falling into the trap of what I call *marketing technopia*. This term is a derivative of the expression *marketing myopia*, which was coined by marketing guru Theodore Levitt in a 1960 essay published in the *Harvard Business Review*. Marketing myopia refers to the condition in which a company or organization loses sight of its real business or mandate. To explain marketing myopia, Levitt uses the example of railroad companies at the turn of the last century which believed they were simply in the "railroad" business. They didn't see that they were really in the "transportation" business.

Because of this shortsightedness (myopia), they failed to anticipate and capitalize on the emergence of trucks, automobiles, and other transportation technology.

While most marketing people now guard against marketing myopia, thanks to the warnings of Theodore Levitt, they're now in danger of falling into another trap — *marketing technopia*. Companies that suffer from this affliction marvel at the wonders of personal computers, modems, Web browsers, voice mail systems, cellular telephones, and the wealth of other gadgets and gizmos. But in their wonderment, they have lost sight of their most important asset — the customer.

Consider these examples of marketing technopia. Have you ever spent 15 minutes trying to reach a department of a large company by voice mail? Have you ever been stuck in a long lineup at a store because the computer was down? Have you ever been told your account has been canceled because of computer error? Of course you have. In each case, the company has chosen to sacrifice the quality of their customer service by using digital technology to cut costs and increase efficiency. And as companies lay off more people and bring in more computers, it's only going to get worse.

This book was written to help turn the tide against marketing technopia. To achieve this, everyone in business must move in two seemingly opposite directions at once. They must selectively choose the digital marketing tools that are appropriate, while keeping the best interests of the customer in mind at all times. After all, what is the point in using digital technology if it turns off your customers?

* * *

Strategic Marketing for the Digital Age is helpful for anyone involved in marketing a product or service. Whether you're the marketing director of a multinational consumer products company or the owner of a single retail store, you'll benefit from the information in this book. It will help you understand digital technology and how it can be used for marketing, and most importantly, it outlines a step-by-step process for developing your own strategic digital marketing program. The entire process is based on the Strategic Digital Marketing Model, which I developed and refined over the past 17 years, working with companies large and small.

This book will also be useful for students of marketing who are interested in combining their studies in classical marketing with the new world of digital marketing. I look in detail at how digital technology — and the digital marketing environment it has fostered — affects the four key areas of marketing: Product Strategy, Pricing Strategy, Distribution Channels, and Promotional Strategy.

In all of this discussion, I will bring you back constantly to the customer. What technology do your customers want to use? Will they feel their privacy is being invaded by digital database records and online research tools? What products do they want to buy online, and what services will they pay for in cyberspace? All of these questions pertaining to the customer will be explored and discussed.

OVERVIEW OF CHAPTERS

Strategic Marketing for the Digital Age is a guide to the world of digital marketing. The book is comprised of 16 chapters divided into five sections. You can follow step by step the ideas laid out in each chapter to create your own digital marketing strategy. Here's a synopsis.

Section One: An Introduction to Digital Marketing: In this section, I look at the digital marketing environment (Chapter 2) and explain how the old ways of marketing have become outmoded. Chapter 3 outlines the Strategic Digital Marketing Model which can be used as the basis for your own digital marketing strategy. Chapter 4 explains the basics of digital and online technology, and their applications to marketing.

Section Two: Planning Your Digital Marketing Strategy: In this section, I set out the process for developing your strategy. I look at how to create your digital vision (Chapter 5), how to assess the technical preferences and capabilities of your target market (Chapter 6), and how to start your customer database (Chapter 7). Chapter 8 takes a close look at each of the digital marketing tools such as the World Wide Web, e-mail, interactive voice response (IVR), CD-ROMs, bulletin board systems (BBS), smart cards, and dozens of others. Chapters 9 and 10 present ideas with which you can attract people to your company's digital promotion, and Chapter 11 explains how to set up your digital command center.

Section Three: Running Your Digital Marketing Program: In this section, I suggest ways to launch your digital marketing program (Chapter 12), and how to assess the effectiveness of your program (Chapter 13).

Section Four: The Ethics of Digital Marketing: Chapters 14 and 15 look at the ethics of digital and online marketing, including issues such as privacy protection, data sharing, data security, online transactions, copyright, trademarks, and government regulations.

Section Five: The Future of Digital Marketing: In the final section, I look into the far future when digital marketing will be fully integrated into the economy. The scenarios presented may help spark new ideas that can be helpful today.

* * *

Strategic Marketing for the Digital Age is meant to be a fun book to read. Because we're all pioneers on the threshold of the great digital age, there are many adventures ahead of us. It may be scary as we head out in our cyberspaceships across the digital frontier, but one thing is certain — it isn't going to be boring.

CHAPTER 2

THE DIGITAL MARKETING ENVIRONMENT

"I shall begin at the beginning," said the D.H.C., and the more zealous students recorded his intention in their notebooks: Begin at the beginning. "These," he waved his hand, "are the incubators." And opening an insulated door he showed them racks upon racks of numbered test-tubes... Still leaning against the incubators, he gave them, while the pencils scurried illegibly across the pages, a brief description of the fertilizing process.

Brave New World
Aldous Huxley, 1932

Studying the powerful influence of technology on the social, economic, and political environment — as seen in Huxley's bleak vision of the future — has been one of the hallmarks of science fiction. In our "brave new world" of global computer networks and multimedia, it's important to understand the influence of digital technology on our environment — in this case, the marketing environment.

The way products and services are conceived, manufactured, priced, distributed, and promoted is being changed fundamentally by the use of digital technology. As digital communications tools are introduced into our economy, we're moving out of the mass-marketing environment — driven by communications tools such as magazines, newspapers, radio, television, telephones, and postal delivery — to a marketing environment defined by the use of digital communications tools such as databases, e-mail, online services, smart cards, calling cards, CD-ROMs, interactive telephone systems, fax-on-demand, and a host of other digital tools.

The use of digital technology in the marketing environment does not mean advertising in newspapers and magazines will become obsolete or that direct mail and telemarketing will disappear. It does not mean that market research using focus groups and person-to-person telephone surveys will become unnecessary. These traditional marketing tools will still have a role to play. They will simply become components of a much more complex marketing environment dominated by digital technology.

CHANGES IN THE MARKETING WORLD

The goal of a marketing program is to sell more products or services, and to generate more revenue, and therefore, more profit. Money spent on marketing is risk capital invested in the hope of generating more revenue than the program's cost. The task of the marketer is to use the budget in the most effective and efficient manner possible. The wise marketer is always asking, "How can I get the greatest impact from each marketing dollar invested?" In this day and age, the answer has become, "Use digital technology!"

In a nutshell, digital marketing tools are used because they're less expensive than traditional marketing tools. Conceivably, you can gather more market research data, dollar for dollar, using digital surveys — conducted online or through interactive voice mail — than through telephone or in-person interviews. You can reach a worldwide market on the Internet for the same cost as placing a full-page ad in a trade magazine. You can send out e-mail messages to 10,000 customers for the cost of mailing one letter to a single customer using postal delivery.

Digital technology also allows you to market products and services more effectively. For example, you can:

- Serve the needs of your customers better by using a database to track their preferences and buying patterns.
- Communicate with your customers around the world faster and more easily using e-mail.
- Develop sales leads more effectively by using interactive kiosks in your stores, or by offering an incentive to call a 1-800 consumer line.

These advantages of digital marketing — cost savings and greater effectiveness — do not mean you should abandon all your tried-and-true marketing methods. But you'd be wise to look at digital alternatives because it's likely your competitors are doing so right now.

WHAT MAKES DIGITAL MARKETING DIFFERENT

Before you enter the digital marketing environment, it's important to understand how it differs from the traditional marketing environment. If you understand the general concepts and new principles of marketing fostered by the use of digital technology, you'll be able to think more creatively when you develop your digital marketing strategy.

Digital marketing is spatial, not linear: The traditional marketing environment is fundamentally linear in nature; steps in the process occur one after another. In this environment, for example, a company conducts market research to determine what products and services are wanted or needed by consumers. The researcher also tries to determine what competitors are doing, and what gaps there may be in the marketplace. Using the research findings, the company creates a new product and manufactures a small test run. The products are shipped to stores in a test market, and advertising is placed in local media. Learning about this new product from a TV or radio ad, consumers flock to the stores and buy it. Weeks later, the marketing manager receives a report on sales in the test market, and learns that they are excellent. He reports the good news to the manufacturing manager, who proceeds to make more products. The products are then sold in many other markets, and the cycle continues.

In the traditional marketing environment, one stage follows the other in a logical sequence. Everything happens slowly, and feedback is spread over many months or years. Decisions are based on the information received during the previous stage. If a mistake has been made, it takes a long time before it is detected and fixed; if results are positive, it takes months to realize the success, wasting time and potentially lucrative opportunities.

In contrast, the digital marketing environment is spatial — rather than linear — in nature. In this spatial environment, all the marketing stages happen at the same time. Market research, product development, and customer feedback take place concurrently.

In the digital marketing environment, the customer becomes an integral player in the development of the product. In fact, a customer might actually build the product herself from a wide array of parts provided by the company. Sales reports are generated continuously, available online, and accessible at all times. Extensive market research is not required because new products are introduced inexpensively and tested on small groups of consumers using digital communications tools. If a product fails to generate sales, the money lost is minimal. In fact, even if the new product is unsuccessful, the extensive information gleaned from the marketplace can more than pay for the cost of developing the test product.

Digital promotions are generally nonintrusive: Unless consumers want to access your digital media, they can avoid it easily. Unlike a television ad that suddenly appears on the screen, or a billboard that grabs your attention as you drive down the road, digital marketing media has to generate interest. You have to make your digital information so compelling that consumers will come back again and again of their own accord.

Digital promotions appeal more to reason than emotion: In mass-media traditional advertising, you are forced to appeal to feelings and emotions because you only have a short time (such as a 30-second TV spot) or a limited amount of space (such as a one-page print ad) to convey a message. But digital marketing media is not constrained by these limitations. You can have as much information available as you want without incurring significantly higher costs. As well, digital consumers are usually looking for information, not sales hype. So your digital marketing promotions must appeal to reason and logic if they are going to sustain the long-term interest of your audience.

The hard sell doesn't work in digital marketing: Because digital marketing is nonintrusive and can be avoided by your audience, hard-sell techniques are less effective in the digital marketing environment than they may be in the mass-marketing environment. To get people to enter your digital domain, you need to provide some sort of enticement, some creative program that will draw them to you of their own free will.

For example, you might provide a lot of useful information in a Web site, or on a CD-ROM. This information might have some relationship to your business, but it isn't all about your business. People will access your Web site, or ask for your CD-ROM, because they want to get the information. Once they have entered your digital domain to get this information, you can then begin to develop a relationship with these potential customers. But if you try the hard sell right up front, these digital consumers will move on at the click of a mouse.

THE CUSTOMER IS THE FOCUS

Digital marketing can build better relationships: Although computers have the reputation of being dehumanizing, digital marketing can be used to develop better business relationships with your customers and prospects. By creating ongoing dialogue and interaction, you'll learn more about your customers, and they'll learn more about you. However, there is a temptation to use digital technology to replace the human element. This is a mistake. Digital technology should be used as a way to begin and foster more high-quality one-on-one relationships.

Get to know your customers as individuals: Digital marketing is emerging at the same time as markets are becoming more and more fragmented. We've moved beyond mass marketing (where everyone wears the same black shoes and drives the same black car) and beyond micromarketing (where consumers choose from a wide array of different styles and colors), into the age of individual markets where each of your customers is seen as a unique person with his or her own needs, lifestyles, preferences, and buying patterns. As such, digital marketing should be customer-focused, rather than product-focused.

Constantly gather information about your customers: When marketing in the digital world, you should gather information constantly. If a potential customer calls for a brochure, for example, get as much information as you can about them and enter it directly into your database. If someone comes into your store, ask them some questions and get their name, address, telephone number, and e-mail address, and store the information in a database. If you have a World Wide Web site, ask visitors to enter their e-mail addresses, and answer online questions. If you have an IVR (interactive voice response) system, get your callers to answer a few questions using the keys on their telephone.

Put customer information into a database: One of your primary objectives as a digital marketer is to develop an extensive database containing detailed information about customers and prospects. The database allows you to develop products and services that meet the needs of each individual. It also allows you to communicate effectively with your customers through e-mail, fax and telephone, and in person. In fact, the database is the most important of all the digital marketing tools.

DEVELOP CAPABILITIES, NOT PRODUCTS

Let customers design their own products: In the digital marketing environment, consumers can be intimately involved in the creation of virtually any product or service. They can design their own university courses, their own cars, and their own homes. This means you should develop capabilities rather than products. For example, a bank should strive to expand its ability to deliver more financial services. Rather than focusing on any specific product, the bank should make a wide range of services available and allow customers to put them together in their own way. The job of the digital marketer, then, is to provide customers with:

- enough information to make a knowledgeable buying decision;
- the information they need to assemble the product;
- the component parts from which to choose; and
- the digital tools to actually do the assembly.

CHANGE CHANNELS AND BE DIFFERENT

Sell directly to your customers and eliminate the middleman: In the digital marketing environment, the middleman is no longer needed. As it becomes possible to purchase products and services online, it will no longer be necessary to use wholesalers and retailers to deliver your products to your customers. Digital consumers deal directly with you. You ship the product directly to the consumer. As a digital marketer, your task is to develop creative and effective ways to distribute information about your products and services, not ways to distribute the actual product.

Don't compete on price; be different: As digital communications technology becomes more widespread, it will become harder and harder to compete on price alone. In the digital marketplace, there is almost universal market knowledge. Everyone knows what everyone else is doing. Because digital consumers shop at the speed of light, they know quickly if there is a difference in price between two dealers, and make their purchase accordingly. If you lower your prices, your competitors will know about it and respond to your lead. To compete, you have to provide unique products or services that no one else provides, or offer them in ways that no one else does.

CHOOSE FROM ALL THE DIGITAL MARKETING TOOLS

Even though the use of digital technology is expanding quickly, the proliferation of digital tools in the consumer marketplace is still in its infancy. Most people do not use computers at home. Only a small portion of US and Canadian households have computers equipped with CD-ROM drives. And only a small percentage of the population uses the Internet and the World Wide Web. This is not to say that you should forget about the Internet or CD-ROMs to market your products or service; it's just to say that you should investigate other digital tools that may be more appropriate.

For example, fax and voice mail are based on digital technology and are used extensively by a large segment of the population. Easy-to-use interactive kiosks are now being used extensively in shopping malls and retail stores. Bank machines are used by most people with little or no training. As well, the use of credit cards and, more recently, direct payment cards, is now such an integral part of our lives that few of us realize we are digital consumers when we use these tools.

The general principle is that you can use digital tools in marketing to your customers even if they don't use computers or surf the Web. That's why I don't put all of my emphasis on the Internet and on computers when I discuss digital marketing.

Use the telephone as a digital device: The telephone is a very powerful digital tool because everyone uses one. You can set up an interactive telephone survey that rewards people for answering questions by using their Touch-Tone keys. This information can be entered into a database and used for promotional purposes, so don't forget about the telephone when you're developing your digital marketing strategy.

Use e-mail to communicate better with customers: A number of computer hardware and telephone companies are getting ready to introduce residential telephones that combine voice mail, e-mail, and Web browsing. Using this low-cost device (under $500), you will be able to send and receive e-mail messages — even if you don't know how to use a computer.

When these devices become commonplace, and everyone has an e-mail address, marketers will use e-mail instead of fax, voice mail, and postal delivery, because it is faster, cheaper, and allows the recipient to send a reply quickly and easily. Marketers will, and currently do, use e-mail to send out electronic coupons, newsletters, and sales letters. When the technology advances further, you will be able to send out e-mail containing full-motion video.

Although it will be some time before everyone has an e-mail address, you should start now to add e-mail addresses to your customer and prospect database.

THE CHANGING ROLE OF TRADITIONAL MEDIA

Use traditional advertising to promote your digital media: As digital marketing media becomes more prevalent and functional, traditional advertising media will become more expensive in relative terms, and will therefore take on a different role. In most cases, you will use traditional advertising media to convince people to access your digital marketing promotions.

For example, if you're a travel company, you might use a small ad (the emphasis is on small) in a trade publication to promote your

CD-ROM that contains information about 7,000 ski resorts. The CD-ROM includes software that allows the user to connect to your online database and get up-to-the-minute snow reports, and, of course, to book a vacation. Or perhaps you are an auctioneer of exotic jewelry. You advertise in a fashion magazine about your World Wide Web site that allows you to bid on valuables electronically. In other words, the traditional advertising media is used to promote your digital media, rather than as a way to describe your products and services.

Negotiate the cost of digital marketing on a results-only basis: When a company places an ad in a newspaper or magazine, it is required to pay for the ad even if it attracts few or no responses. In the digital marketing environment, however, the advertiser should not be expected to pay full price if there is no response. This is because the cost of delivering an advertising message the traditional way is expensive, while the digital method is much cheaper.

A magazine, for example, spends a lot of money to produce each issue and deliver it to readers. The advertiser is therefore guaranteed a certain circulation and is required to pay up front for the cost of delivering the message, regardless of the response. However, an Internet Web site provider does not have to spend a lot of money to deliver the message (certainly a fraction of the cost of producing a magazine), so the advertiser should not be expected to pay a set amount regardless of the response.

Because the cost of delivering a digital message is so low, the advertiser should insist on paying only if there are significant consumer enquiries or actual sales generated by the digital promotion. The agency or digital media provider may charge for the costs of the creative development of the program, but the cost of delivering the message might be based on a commission system.

For these reasons, the traditional ways of assessing promotional media do not apply to digital media. Circulation figures, gross rating points (GRP), and total impressions are not relevant to digital media. That's why attempts to assess the popularity of a World Wide Web site — by counting the number of "hits" — are an anachronism. Digital advertisers should be saying: "Who cares how many people saw my site? What did it do for me? How many sales did it generate? How many people left useful information for our database?"

PROVIDE QUALITY CONTENT OR SOMETHING USEFUL

Because digital marketing is generally nonintrusive, you will have to attract people to your company by providing quality content that can't be found anywhere else, or by providing a new way of doing something that makes life better for your customers.

Think public relations, not advertising: I believe digital marketing is more akin to public relations than to advertising. Public relations — or publicity — generates coverage in newspapers, magazines, radio, and television to influence consumer behavior. Successful publicity can be achieved by providing the media with information related to your business, but not necessarily about your business.

For example, if you're a software company, you can send the media news releases about the latest trends in computing, or advice on how to buy the most appropriate software for your company's warehouse. This type of noncommercial information is useful to people, and an editor would be more likely to run an article about it in his newspaper or magazine. If you simply send the media a news release about your new product and how great it is, without any background information, an editor might be less interested, and the possibility of generating media coverage could be diminished.

The same approach works best with digital marketing promotions. You have to provide useful information that will easily attract people. Unlike most advertising, a digital promotion has to be full of interesting content. The mistake we see people making on the Internet is that they set up a World Wide Web site that is simply an advertisement. And in fact, 95 percent of the information being placed on the

Web is simply advertisement. The question to ask is: "If people avoid television advertising by flipping from one station to another, why would they spend time reading your ad on the Internet?"

That's why I think marketers with experience in public relations are much more suited to the task of developing content for the Internet and other digital platforms such as fax-on-demand systems and private online networks. They understand that digital promotions — being nonintrusive and easily avoided — must provide useful information that will attract people of their own free will.

Make your digital content comprehensive: If you are trying to attract people to your digital storefront by providing content, you need to make sure the content is comprehensive, easy to find, relevant, and current. For example, a law firm can publish a CD-ROM containing advice on 500 legal matters faced by small businesses. A CD-ROM of this nature will be much more popular than a CD-ROM about the history of the law firm.

Another way to attract people to your digital media is to provide a database of information that can be searched based on different criteria. For example, if you are an antique dealer, you can set up an online database listing all the antique furniture for sale in North America. Or you can offer a database listing all the antique clocks for sale in the world. People will be attracted to this database because it is a comprehensive list. They will be less interested if the database only contains listings from your own store, or your own city. In other words, the less comprehensive your database, the less effective it will be in attracting interested consumers.

Make life easier, faster, or less expensive: In the initial euphoria over the Internet's World Wide Web, only a few astute companies realized that the most powerful marketing value of this new medium is its ability to provide a faster, easier, and less expensive way to do something useful. For example, Federal Express established a Web site so you can order courier pickups through the Internet. As well, you can check on the status of your other packages and get a current account statement — all directly from your computer! Other major courier companies such as Purolator and UPS followed suit within months with their own online systems.

A Toronto-based company called PaymentLink beat out the major Canadian banks and launched an online bill payment service on the Internet that allows you to pay your bills with a few clicks of a mouse. No more cheques, envelopes, or trips to the bank machine! The system allows you to pay your bills 24 hours a day, seven days a week, and sends you a confirmation the next day by e-mail.

Ticket Master, the event ticket agency, set up a site that allows you to buy tickets online for major sports and cultural events. When you access the site, you can pick the event you want, and call up a seating plan of the stadium or concert hall. The available seats are shown blinking on the screen. You simply choose the seats you want and click to order!

Each of these examples demonstrates the real marketing power of online technology, which is to provide a faster and easier way to do a transaction. By removing intermediaries, you give the customer more control over the process. As well, both you and the customer save time and money.

So, when you are developing your digital marketing strategy, consider how you can use the technology to help your customers deal with your company in less time and for less money.

Improve Customer Service: Companies that use digital technology to automate their marketing processes free up people to deal with customers in a more relaxed and meaningful way. For example, the use of the ABM (Automated Banking Machine) has freed up tellers from handling the more run-of-the-mill transactions such as depositing cheques and withdrawing money. Bank employees can now spend their time working with customers face-to-face on more important matters such as loan applications and mutual fund sales. Of course, many banks have simply laid off employees replaced by automation, but the smart ones will use the technology to improve customer service.

WHAT YOU NEED TO DO

Be proactive: One attraction of setting up a World Wide Web site is that it's easy. You hire an Internet consultant, pay some money, and voilà, you have a Web site and a presence on the Internet. Then you sit back and wait for the telephone calls and e-mail messages to start pouring in from interested buyers. Sound too good to be true? It is. The passive approach won't work.

With digital marketing, you have to be proactive. You have to make things happen. My favorite story about digital marketing is an old one. It is the story about how American Airlines (AA) transformed its business and totally eclipsed the competition. Back in the late 1970s, American Airlines developed an automated reservation system called Sabre. To get the travel agents to use it, they proactively gave the large travel agencies a free computer and trained agents how to order airline tickets using this new technology. Because the system was faster, easier, and less expensive, the agents started using it all the time, and they started ordering the majority of their flights from American Airlines.

Well, you can imagine how the other airlines reacted. They immediately set about developing their own online ordering systems. But when the rival airlines tried to get the agents to use another computer to order flights from them, the agents balked. They were used to using the AA system and didn't want another computer on their desk. "Couldn't you simply get AA to put your information on their system?" the travel agents asked. And that's what the other airlines were forced to do. They had to go to AA, hat in hand, and beg them to put their information on the AA system. AA agreed, but asked for a commission on every ticket ordered through the system.

Today, American Airlines makes more money from its reservation system and from the commissions on sales of its competitors' flights than it does from its airline operations. In 1989, the value of the Sabre system was assessed at more than $1 billion. As well, American Airlines has now made its Sabre system available online so customers can order their flights directly and avoid the travel agent all together.

All this has occurred because American Airlines decided to proactively connect its best customers to their system, even if it required giving away free computers and training each agent.

My own proactive strategy worked as well, if on a smaller scale. In 1990, I decided to set up a private online network for my marketing communications company which would electronically link me to my clients and my suppliers. I found an excellent bulletin board system software program called "FirstClass™" and connected my Macintosh to the telephone system with two modems. I then went to my customers and hooked up their computers to modems and installed the needed software. In some cases, I gave the client the modem. I did the same with my key suppliers such as writers, designers, printers, and prepress companies.

Within a few months, a majority of my business was being conducted online, and the productivity gains were incredible. As well, my clients were happier because it was easier to communicate with me, and to transfer computer files back and forth. By proactively connecting clients to my company's computer system, I forged a much more solid bond with them, and improved my level of customer service.

Both of these examples illustrate the value of proactively using online and digital technology to connect your best customers to your company. For example, if you run a business stationery and supplies store, a good strategy would be to develop a system that allows your best clients to order supplies from you using their computer. Your salespeople would be trained how to install the software, and how to train the customer to use it. Once your system is being used regularly by customers, you will have a tremendous advantage over your competition. In fact, customers will be unlikely to switch to a competitor, or use a competitor occasionally, because it will be much easier and faster to order from you. So get proactive — don't think of digital marketing as a passive armchair activity.

Find the hidden digital assets in your company: Most organizations already possess digital marketing assets, even if they don't use the Internet. If you have been using a computer to bill your customers, you already have a database of information that is useful for marketing purposes. The database can tell you who your best customers are, what products and services they buy, and at what times and in what volume — along with their addresses and telephone numbers.

You can use this data to analyze your customers' past purchasing habits and predict their future patterns. As well, this database of information may be valuable to other people, who might want to reach your customers to sell them something totally unrelated to your products and services. Just think what an asset your database would be if you proactively developed a much larger and more sophisticated one.

Enlist the participation of everyone in your company: Your first step should be to connect everyone within the company to e-mail, and then set up an e-mail connection to the Internet. In this way, everyone in your company can be reached electronically by your customers. If the customer has a question, she should be able to send an e-mail directly to your president. Because digital technology such as e-mail makes it easy and inexpensive to communicate around the world, everyone in your company must be prepared to communicate with the customer.

Make a long-term commitment: Once you have started a digital marketing program, you must be prepared to constantly improve and change the information you are providing. If you have a World Wide Web site, you should be prepared to change the information monthly, if not daily. It is not sufficient to simply put up a Web site and then leave it for six months. If you want people to return to your site on a regular basis, you have to give them something new to do, read, or see.

Develop a vision and have patience: If you develop a long-range vision for digital marketing, your company will have an excellent chance to emerge in the next century as a leader in your industry. If you have the foresight and patience to pull together all the digital marketing tools and processes in an integrated manner, the results will be significantly better than if you simply set up a Web site and hope for the best.

More Questions than Answers: In this chapter, I've tried to illustrate some of the new digital marketing principles. However, these are general principles. The job now is to focus on your own personal situation. In the coming chapters, the following topics will be discussed:

- How can I use digital technology to achieve my business objectives?
- Why should I use digital technology for marketing purposes?
- What are the advantages for me to use digital tools over traditional marketing tools such as advertising, public relations, sales promotion, direct marketing, and telemarketing?
- What digital tools do my customers currently use? What proactive strategy could I employ to get them to use the ones I use or plan to use?
- To what new markets does digital technology give me access? Can I access new markets previously beyond my reach or resources?
- How can I use digital technology to track my customers' buying habits, preferences, tastes, and opinions?
- How can I best assess the impact of my digital marketing program?

I will now look closely at the Strategic Digital Marketing Model, which I developed to establish standard principles and guidelines for digital marketing.

CHAPTER 3

THE STRATEGIC DIGITAL MARKETING MODEL

The Galactic Empire was falling... It had been falling for centuries before one man became really aware of that fall. That man was Hari Seldon, the man who represented the one spark of creative effort left among the gathering decay. He developed and brought to its highest pitch the science of psychohistory.

Foundation and Empire
Isaac Asimov, 1952

In his celebrated *Foundation Trilogy*, Isaac Asimov tells the story of the Galactic Empire, a future civilization threatened with extinction. The hero of the book, Hari Seldon, uses the science of psychohistory to control the future by predicting it using statistical probability. It's a fascinating idea — predicting and controlling the future using science.

Imagine if you could do the same with digital marketing. By using a foundation of universal laws and principles, you could develop your own digital marketing strategy. And as you were going along, you could periodically refer back to these principles to see if you were still on the right track. As we all know, it's very hard to build an empire until you have built a proper foundation.

That's why I developed a universal framework called the Strategic Digital Marketing (SDM) Model. It can be used by any size of business, in any industry, with any type of product and service. In fact, even a one-person business can employ most of the digital tools and processes used by the largest corporation. That's one of the great advantages of the digital revolution — it gives almost every business access to the same technology.

START WITH A STRATEGY

This book was written to help you develop your own strategy for digital marketing. The SDM Model begins, therefore, with an emphasis on the need for *strategic planning* before anything else. I've seen, time and time again, marketers put all their money and effort into building an elaborate World Wide Web site, with little or no strategic thinking first. In the final analysis, they end up with the equivalent of a beautifully designed and expensive brochure. People come to their site, look around, realize it's just another advertisement, and leave. The Web software records thousands and thousands of hits, but nothing happens. No increased sales. No increased knowledge of the customer. Nothing.

So start with a strategy. Go through the steps outlined in this book first. For example, think through your need for a Web site. Do your customers actually use the Internet? Remember, as of 1996, only about 20 percent of the population use the Internet, and a smaller portion of them use the World Wide Web. Perhaps other digital tools such as a private online network (BBS) or a point-of-sale smart card program would be more effective for marketing your service or product.

THE FOUNDATION OF YOUR EMPIRE

Growth based on higher productivity: Growth is the primary objective of the SDM Model. During the past ten years — as we have made the transition from a mass-market, manufacturing-based economy to the digital, information-based economy — the emphasis has been on restructuring and downsizing. The time has now come to put the emphasis on growth based on the productivity gains made possible by the use of digital technology.

Growth will be realized by increasing sales while keeping a lid on costs, especially the costs of marketing. Sales will increase either by attracting the attention of new customers, in new or existing markets, or by getting your existing customers to spend more of their money on *your* goods and services rather than those of your competitors. While this emphasis on growth may seem trite, it's important to keep focused on the key objective — increased profits — rather than be dazzled by the technology itself.

One-to-one customer focus: Individual customers are the heart of the SDM Model. Using digital technology and one-to-one contact, your objective is to learn as much as you can about your customers and prospective customers. With this information, you can develop products and services to meet their specific needs and communicate with them on a regular, consistent basis.

Micromarket segments: While getting to know each customer on a one-to-one basis is the primary focus of SDM, you need to segment them into small micromarkets or segments. By identifying each of these micromarkets, you can plan your marketing strategy more effectively. For example, if you are a financial services company, you might divide your market into seven segments, as follows:

- Top 20 percent (Best Customers)
- Young Singles
- Married *without* Children
- Married *with* Children
- High-income Earners
- Close to Retirement
- Retired

You then develop unique products, services, and digital marketing promotions for each of these segments. In fact, with the ease that digital information is moved around, you can develop specific marketing strategies for an unlimited number of micromarket segments. However, keeping your micromarkets down to a manageable number — say three for a small business, and around ten for a large company — is advisable at first.

Central database: A database is the central digital tool of the SDM Model. The database is used to store the information about your customers and prospects: what they buy, when they buy, what they like and dislike about your products, where they live, their e-mail address, their fax number. Developed properly, this database will become the most valuable asset in your company. The database is stored on a central computer, whether it be a midframe IBM AS/400 computer owned by a major retail chain, or a stand-alone PC running in your home office.

Gather information using digital tools: Digital marketing tools such as the Internet, interactive voice response, retail point-of-sale systems, and smart cards are used to gather information for the database. Your World Wide Web site, for example, may promote a contest that requires contestants to fill in a detailed survey about their likes and dislikes. The data compiled by the online survey is then fed directly into the database. Or you might set up a Customer Loyalty Program in which your best customers use a smart card when they shop in your store. Every time someone uses the card, the information is fed into a database which keeps track of what they are buying, and when and how much money is being spent. In another scenario, your private online network — available to only your biggest customers — keeps track of what information they access and allows them to purchase products and services online.

In other words, there is no point in using digital tools, such as a World Wide Web site, if you are not gathering specific information. Even if you get a million "hits" on your site, it's virtually useless unless the people leave some information about themselves before they move on. So make sure you link your digital tools to a database. At the very least, I recommend you encourage people to leave their e-mail address or fax number. You can then enter this data into a database and use it for future outgoing communications such as a newsletter or an e-mail bulletin.

Under the SDM Model, all other digital devices are secondary to the database, including the Internet. There is little point in having a World Wide Web site, or a 1-800 voice-response system, unless the device is used to collect information for your central database.

YOUR DIGITAL DOMAIN

Your Digital Domain is the hypothetical digital environment where you and your customers come together. Your goal as a digital marketer is to attract customers and prospects to your Digital Domain using unique promotions.

Give your customers an incentive to access your Digital Domain: Under the SDM Model, your digital marketing promotions are designed to encourage the people in your target market(s) to access your Digital Domain on an ongoing basis. This can be done by offering:

- a financial incentive (such as $20 off long-distance calling);
- an intellectual incentive (such as the complete collection of 19th-century English literature on CD-ROM);
- a functional incentive (such as a way to order groceries or couriers online); and
- an entertaining incentive (by providing access to audio and video clips of popular entertainers).

Given the right reason, your prospective customers will access your Digital Domain regularly and provide you with the information you need from them. It will also give you a chance to expose them to information about your company's products and services. As I said in Chapter 2, digital marketing is essentially nonintrusive. You have to develop content and functionality that makes life easier, less expensive, more interesting, or more fun. Remember, if you make only the minimal effort and simply put your advertising online, no one will be interested.

Ongoing communication and constant feedback: The digital marketing process requires a commitment to ongoing communication with your customers and prospects. In fact, digital technology provides you with a way to communicate quickly, easily, and inexpensively, on a one-to-one basis. For example, when you gather information from your retail smart card program, you should get the telephone number, fax number, and e-mail address from each customer. Ask them if they would like to receive regular information from your company and how they would like to receive it — by telephone, fax, or e-mail.

Based on the information you have in your database, you can send out regular e-mail and fax bulletins about sales and special promotions. For the people who choose to receive information by telephone, you can use electronic telemarketing technology to call your customers and leave voice messages (or you can have a "real" person make the calls). When these outbound messages are being made, the goal is once again to gather additional information and feedback for your database. Are you interested in this promotion? What are your needs at this time? Do you buy our competitors' products? What do you prefer about their products?

It's spatial, not linear: The SDM process is spatial, not linear. As I discussed in Chapter 2, all the processes of digital marketing happen concurrently. While you're promoting your sale by e-mail, you're conducting market research by asking your customers questions. Based on the information received from your customers, you can quickly change your products, services, prices, or distribution system.

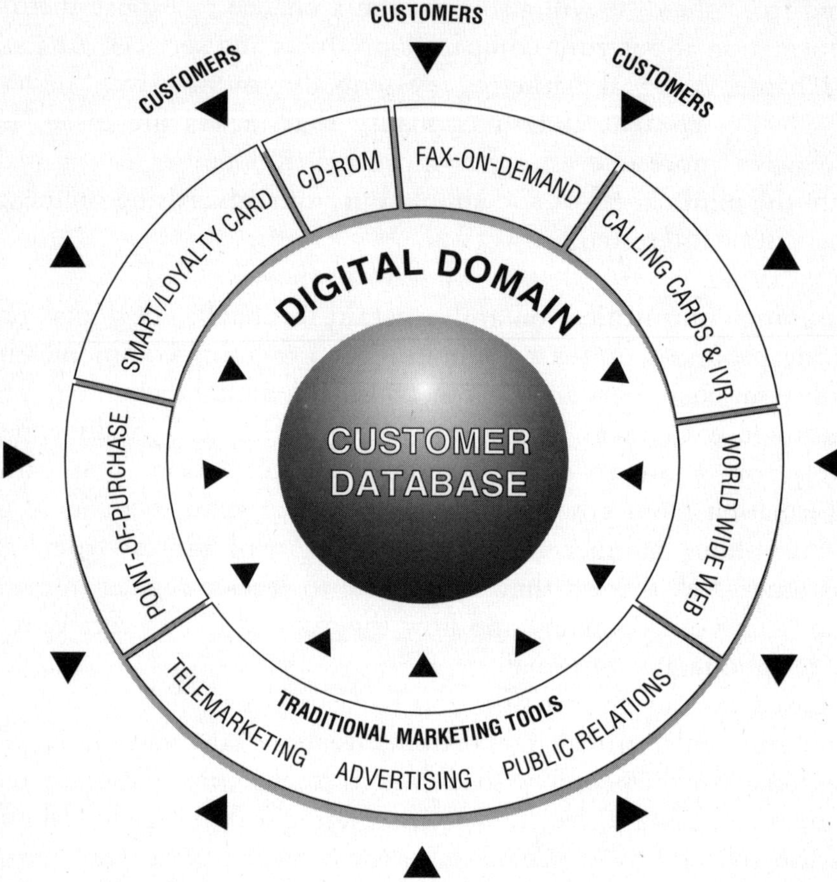

Stage 1: Build Customer Database: Use digital and traditional marketing tools to gather information about your existing customers, and enter the data into a relational database. The environment surrounding your database is called your Digital Domain.

Strategic Digital Marketing Model

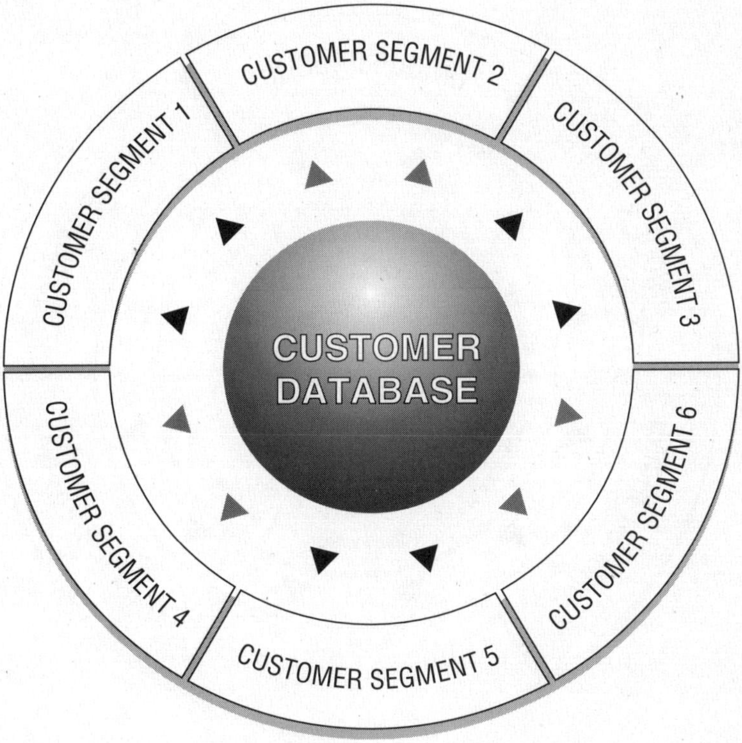

Stage 2: Create Customer Segments: Divide your customer base into segments based on common characteristics. For example, you can divide your customer base into seven segments: Top 20 percent (Best Customers), Young Singles, Married without Children, Married with Children, High-income Earners, Close to Retirement, and Retired.

Strategic Digital Marketing Model

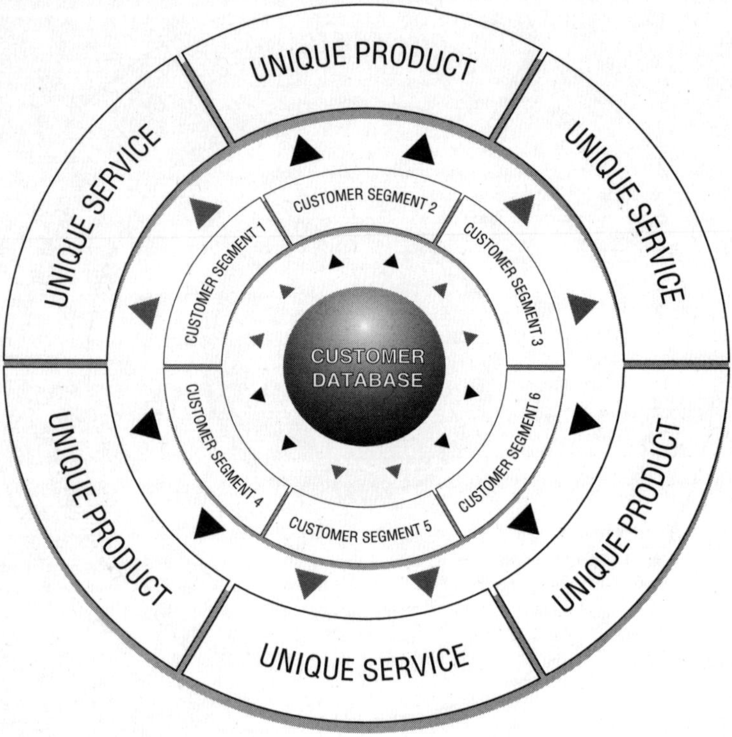

Stage 3: Develop Unique Products and Services: Create new and innovative digital products and services for each of your customer segments.

Strategic Digital Marketing Model

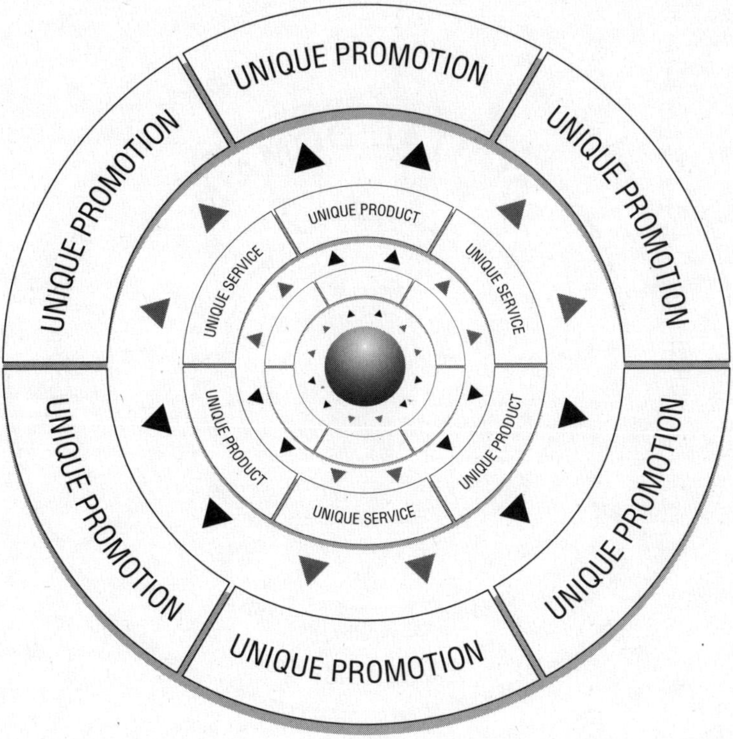

Stage 4: Create Unique Digital Promotions: Dream up digital promotions for each unique product and service. To attract people of their own free will to your digital domain, make your digital promotions useful, entertaining, functional or novel.

Strategic Digital Marketing Model

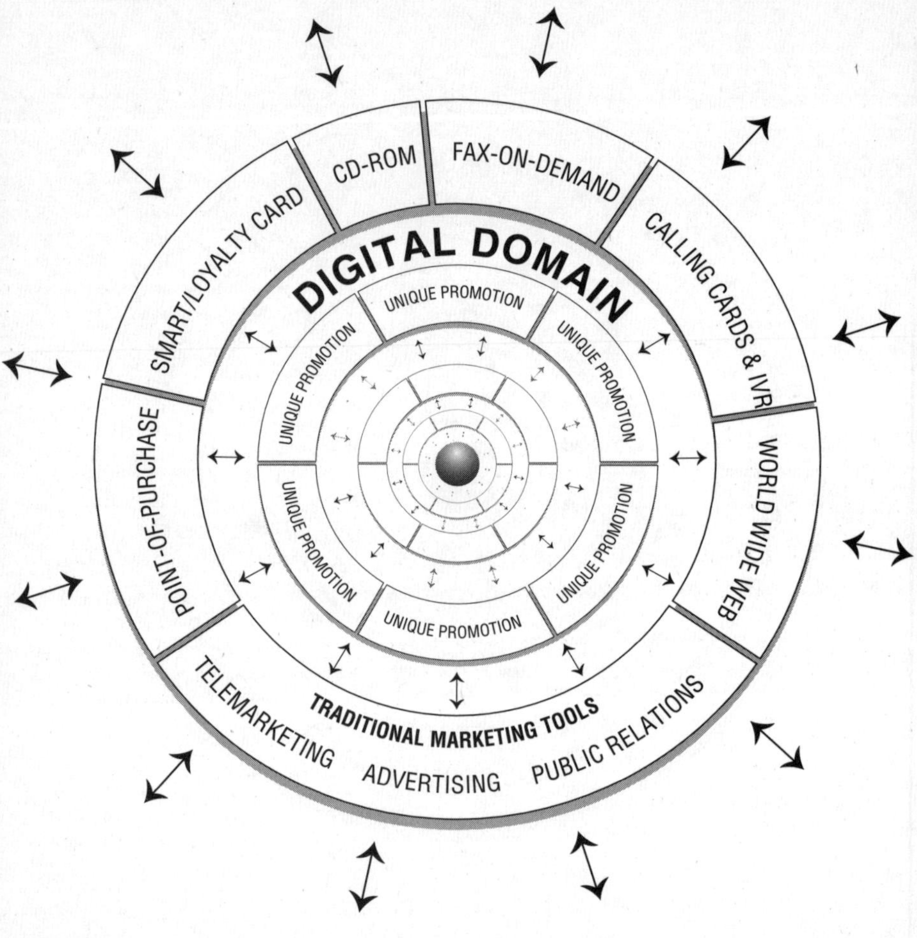

Stage 5: Use Digital and Online Tools to Communicate: Your customers and prospects will access your digital promotions using digital and online technology, and leave information about themselves for your database. Once you have customers and prospects in your database, use digital tools to communicate with them in a regular basis.

Strategic Digital Marketing Model

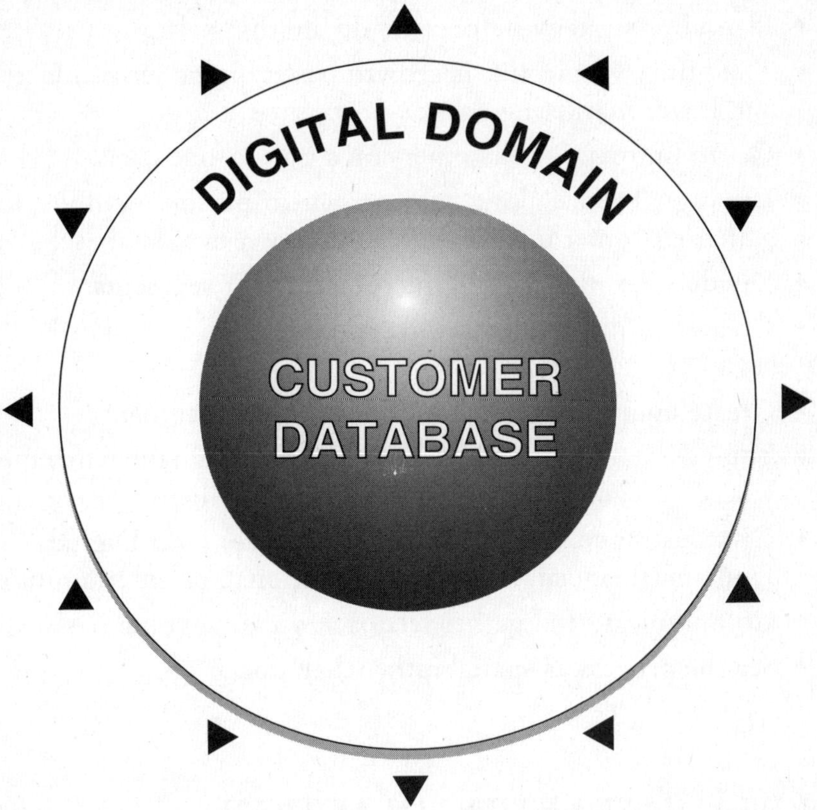

Stage 6: Expand Your Digital Domain: As your customer database grows, the size of your Digital Domain will also expand. You will create additional market segments, develop more digital products and services, initiate new digital promotions, and add new digital tools and capabilities.

Strategic Digital Marketing Model

Recap: To summarize, the Strategic Digital Marketing Model is based on these principles:

- Plan your strategy before you do anything else.
- The primary objective is growth based on higher productivity and lower marketing costs.
- Get to know your customers on a one-to-one basis.
- Use digital tools, along with person-to-person methods, to gather customer information and store it in a database.
- Divide your market into micromarkets or segments.
- Create unique products and services for each market segment.
- Create unique digital promotions for each segment.
- Your Digital Domain is the hypothetical digital environment where you and your customers come together.
- Give customers a good incentive to access your Digital Domain (financial, intellectual, functional, or entertaining).
- Communicate and gather feedback on an ongoing basis.
- See the process as spatial rather than linear.

DIGITAL MARKETING IN ACTION

Now, let's look at the Strategic Digital Marketing Model in action. Here are three hypothetical scenarios:

> **Walrus Design**, a one-woman graphic design shop run by Veronica Byte from her farm in Ontario.
>
> **The Jolly Mutineer Restaurants**, a chain of British-style pubs located across the United States. Susan Mouse is the person in charge of the chain's franchise development and marketing department.

Toys Terrific, an exporter and manufacturer of children's toys located in Rochester, New York. The marketing for Toys Terrific is handled by Don Data.

Walrus Design

Annual Sales	—	$450,000
Annual Profit	—	$200,000
Number of Employees	—	1
Customer Base	—	20 to 25 regular clients
Years in Business	—	7
Key Product/Service	—	Computer-aided interior and exterior design of retail stores
Owner/Operator	—	Veronica Byte

Veronica Byte is a very talented graphic designer and astute businessperson. She started Walrus Design seven years ago after leaving a large retail design firm located in Vancouver. She decided to set up shop in Ontario on a farm. From her home office, Veronica is able to service a high-quality group of clients located across North America. She also has two clients in Hong Kong and one in Italy. Along with a team of other designers (all working from their own offices across the continent), Veronica designs retail storefronts and interiors. Her work has won several industry awards. She is able to generate a profit of more than $200,000 a year from sales of approximately $450,000.

Veronica uses the Strategic Digital Marketing Model to attract new clients. She has divided her market into three segments: Large Chain Stores, Single Store Owners, and Franchisers. Veronica has a relational database on her computer which contains information about her clients as well as more than 2,000 potential clients around the world.

About three years ago, she launched a digital promotion to help retailers get the information they need to run their businesses more effectively. She created the well-known World Wide Web site called Retail World that lists thousands of the resources available on the Internet that are of interest to retailers including industry reports, case studies, merchandising ideas, government regulations, and franchise opportunities. The site features a Chat Room, where retailers can post questions to each other about the retail industry.

Retail World has an interactive survey visitors must complete before being allowed to use the site. About ten retailers complete the survey each week and the information is uploaded automatically to Veronica's database. At any time, Veronica can access the database to see who has been online, what type of retail operation they have, how long they've been in business, and what type of information they're interested in.

Every four months, Veronica writes a two-page industry report on retail design. The report is distributed automatically by fax and e-mail broadcast software linked to her database. The report is well received because it contains useful information. After sending out each report, Veronica usually receives four or five calls from retailers around the world. They are looking for additional information, which Veronica provides if she can. During this process, she is constantly developing better one-to-one relationships with a select group of people on her database. In fact, there is never a shortage of work or calls for proposals. Her digital marketing program is constantly bringing her new work as well as constantly expanding the size of her potential market.

In addition to her Retail World digital marketing promotion, Veronica has created a private online network that links her suppliers and her clients. The network is run on easy-to-use bulletin board service (BBS) software. During the past three years, Veronica has been proactive in connecting her suppliers and clients to this private online network. Each of her clients uses the system to send and receive e-mail and digital files when they're working with Veronica. In fact, the working environment of her clients is seamlessly linked to her office and to her suppliers. Veronica merely controls the flow of the digital information from her subcontractors to her clients.

In this way, Veronica can generate more than $200,000 in profit from only $450,000 in sales. Digital technology has kept her overhead and marketing costs very low. Her World Wide Web site runs on a server located in downtown Toronto and costs her about $300 a month to maintain. Her BBS system is operated by a service provider in Montreal and costs her $30 per year, per user. She also pays about $30 a month for unlimited access to the Internet. Veronica's total marketing costs are about $8,000 a year.

The future looks bright for Veronica and Walrus Design. Several retail industry publications and trade show organizers would like to rent her database list. She is considering developing a CD-ROM version of Retail World, which will be sold through a publisher. She is also gaining new higher-quality clients on a regular basis — all thanks to Strategic Digital Marketing.

The Jolly Mutineer Restaurants

Annual Sales	—	$125 million
Annual Profit	—	$12 million
Number of Employees	—	1,200
Number of Locations	—	45
Customer Base	—	2.5 million customers annually
Years in Business	—	14
Key Product/Service	—	Franchiser of Jolly Mutineer Restaurants
Marketing Director	—	Susan Mouse

When Susan Mouse took over the job of marketing at Jolly Mutineer Restaurants, the department was in a shambles. After 12 years of growth, sales were falling off at most of the chain's locations. Repeat business had fallen from an average of 20 visits a year to fewer than six. New competitors — including the fast-growing chain of Super Sirloin Steakhouses — were stealing business away at a steady rate. Something had to be done — and fast. At the last franchisers' meeting, a group of disgruntled owners threatened to mutiny and sell off their locations.

Luckily, Susan Mouse had recently read *Strategic Marketing for the Digital Age*. Using the Strategic Digital Marketing Model, Susan developed a strategy that brought in more new customers and encouraged her existing customers to visit the restaurants more often. Her first step was to create a database at head office to keep track of customers. Susan divided her customer base into five segments:

- Top-of-the-Mast
- Family Passengers
- Little Mutineers
- Stowaways
- Walk-the-Plank

The Top-of-the-Mast segment is comprised of the restaurant's best customers, people who return time and time again. Family Passengers and Little Mutineers are those families and children who come to the restaurant regularly. Stowaways are the customers who only visit the restaurant rarely, while Walk-the-Plank customers are those who everyone at the Jolly Mutineer, for various reasons, wish would dine somewhere else.

To encourage repeat business, Susan created the Jolly Mutineer Club aimed at the Top-of-the-Mast and Family Passenger customers. Membership in the club entitles customers to discounts on meals, special prizes, invitations to exclusive parties, and a subscription to the Jolly Mutineer newsletter. As well, members also receive air mile points for each restaurant visit.

To join the club, customers fill in an application form at one of the restaurants (for which they receive $10 off their bill). The form, complete with the customer's name, address, fax, and e-mail address, is sent to head office where the information is entered into the database. At three of the larger Jolly Mutineer locations, there are interactive, touch-screen kiosks where customers can enter the information directly into the database.

Each week, more than 6,000 customers join the club. More than 25 percent of them provide their e-mail address, and 55 percent of them provide a fax number. Each month, Susan sends out a message to members providing them with a discount on lunch and dinner menu items. As well, the database also keeps track of birthdays and anniversaries of members so telemarketers can call members to arrange reservations for special events.

To attract new customers, Susan developed the Jolly Mutineer Sweepstakes Program aimed at more than one million households across the country. Each household received a letter inviting them to call a 1-800 number to enter a contest to win a Caribbean cruise. To enter the contest, the contestant keys in a unique personal identification number shown on the letter and answers a series of questions. Twenty-five of the PIN numbers identify the winners. Runners-up receive other prizes, and every contestant receives a 50-percent-off coupon by mail the following week. In all cases, the contestants need to provide information about themselves in order to participate in the contest. Of course, all this information is entered into the database.

Since the program's start-up a year ago, the Jolly Mutineer database has grown to more than 485,000 names. Repeat business is up by 20 percent, and new customers are up by 35 percent. Increased revenue has more than paid for the cost of the marketing program and indeed has returned a healthy profit. As well, three other companies are interested in renting the database from the Jolly Mutineer, although the company has yet to figure out the ethical ramifications of sharing its list.

Toys Terrific

Annual Sales	—	$425 million
Annual Profit	—	$36 million
Number of Employees	—	870
Years in Business	—	15
Key Product/Service	—	Educational toys for children
Marketing Director	—	Don Data

During the past 15 years, Toys Terrific has built up a multimillion dollar business selling educational toys using its catalogue distributed to schools and households across North America. But during the past three years, the company's share of the market has dropped significantly as two new competitors have entered the industry. Don Data, the new marketing director at Toys Terrific, was given the job to fight back.

Don's first move was to revitalize the company's customer database. In fact, the company had three different databases — one for the ordering department, one for the marketing department, and one for the customer enquiry department. Don brought all of these separate databases together and eliminated the errors and redundancies. Now the company has one central database which can be accessed and updated from every department. (For example, if someone's address or telephone is changed, it is now only necessary to change one record, rather than three, which was the case before the databases were combined. This is one of the major advantages of a relational database, which I will discuss later in greater detail.)

With the database in place, Don began to add the first of many digital input devices — an interactive voice-response system. In advertising placed in major consumer magazines, parents were invited to call a 1-800 number to enter a Scholarship Fund Contest. After the caller had answered a series of questions, her name was entered into the contest to win a full four-year university scholarship for her child. The contest was instantly successful. More than 195,000 parents called the contest line in the first two months. And more importantly, detailed information about the parents and their children was entered automatically into the company's database.

Don then moved into cyberspace and created a World Wide Web site. The site contains the Toys Terrific catalogue, and allows you to purchase the products online using your credit card. You can enter the contest by filling out an online questionnaire. In addition, the site contains a vast library of information of interest to parents, along with an extensive list of other sites on the Internet that pertain to childhood education. As the site has become more popular, Don has added a chat function, and schedules weekly online forums, which allow teachers and parents to discuss education issues. As was the case with the interactive voice-response system, all the information gathered at the site is entered into the company's customer database.

Within a year, the company's database has grown to more than one million names across North America. In addition to the person's name, address, and telephone/fax/e-mail numbers, the database contains extensive information about the person, including number of children, age of children, and the special interests and hobbies of the children. Using this information, Don has divided his market into three different segments and developed specific promotional material for each segment. Three different catalogues were created: one for families with children under five years old, one for children between five and 12, and one for teenagers. These specially targeted catalogues are sent out by mail, fax, and e-mail on a quarterly basis.

To develop a better relationship with teachers and students at elementary schools, Don created the Toys Terrific Online Network. (In contrast to a World Wide Web site, the private BBS is only accessible to students and teachers who have an account and the required software. It does not require an Internet account to use it.)

When making a sales call, Toys Terrific salespeople install the network software on computers in classrooms and school libraries. Students are encouraged to sign up for an account on the network by joining the E-mail Pal Club which matches up children of similar ages and interests. Teachers and school administrators are also encouraged to join the network to participate in educational forums and discussion groups.

In addition to information about Toys Terrific, the network features other information from textbook publishers, school equipment suppliers, student travel agencies, and other companies and organizations of interest to elementary school teachers and students. Of course, the Toys Terrific Online Network features a number of surveys and entry forms linked directly to the company's database.

All these initiatives — the customer database, the 1-800 Scholarship Fund Contest, the Internet Web site, and the private online network are integrated. The complete program gives Toys Terrific a strong competitive advantage in the marketplace. Both competitors still rely on their print-based catalogue to generate sales. Toys Terrific has regained a large part of its lost market share and has substantially increased sales. It has also lowered its marketing costs by cutting down on the number of catalogues it prints, and the amount of traditional advertising it purchases. And, it is providing valuable services to its community.

THE BEGINNING OF YOUR EMPIRE

Each of these companies has successfully used digital technology to achieve its business objectives. They have used the digital tools most appropriate for the people in their market. They've combined a number of different tools in an integrated process. They've used creative campaigns to get their customers and prospects to access their digital sites. And, most importantly, they've used these digital tools to find out more about their customers, and then put this information into a database.

In essence, the Strategic Digital Marketing Model is quite simple. The goal is to gather more information about your customers and prospects. With this information, you can communicate with them more effectively, and provide them with custom-tailored products and services. At all times you are using digital technology to communicate better, and to develop closer relationships with your customers. And in addition, you are increasing the effectiveness of your promotional efforts while controlling your costs.

* * *

Before we begin to develop your own digital marketing strategy, we will first take a look at the fundamentals of digital and online technology in Chapter 4.

CHAPTER 4

THE POWER OF DIGITAL TECHNOLOGY

Pump Station One was lacking in the glisten of the later stations but it was the granddaddy of them all, of the entire chain that girdled the planet even though the entire technology was only a couple of decades old. No major technological advance had ever caught hold so rapidly and so entirely and why not? It meant free energy without limit and without problems. It was the Santa Claus and the Aladdin's lamp of the whole world.

The Gods Themselves
Isaac Asimov, 1972

When Isaac Asimov wrote *The Gods Themselves* in 1972, the Internet was already a decade old, yet few people had ever heard of it outside of military and academic circles. In the book, a way has been found to draw unlimited energy from a parallel universe. The benefits of the new technology are so great that few people take the time to understand how it works and what its true implications are to the world. Asimov could have been writing about online and digital technology. In the 1990s, everyone has been rushing to embrace these new digital wonders, yet few people really understand the fundamentals of the technology.

I believe you need to understand the basics of digital and online technology before you develop your digital marketing strategy. From my experience, most people have only a fragmented comprehension of the subject. They understand something about the Internet, computers, and databases, but no one has ever explained to them the whole thing from the start to finish in simple terms. This chapter is an attempt to fill in any holes there might be in your understanding of basic online and digital technology.

THE BASICS OF BITS AND BYTES

In the digital world, you are either number 1 or a 0. Everything that is stored on a computer — a story, a picture, a movie, or a sound — is actually made up of 1s and 0s. For example, the letter "B" in a word processing document is actually stored on your computer as something like "10101101." Every time you press the letter B on your keyboard, the computer places it into memory as 10101101.

A single binary digit — either 1 or 0 — is known as a *bit*. A string of eight 1s and 0s, such as our example 10101101, is known as a *byte*. One thousand (1,000) bytes is equal to one *kilobyte*, and one million (1,000,000) bytes is equal to one *megabyte*.

Text characters such as the letter B take up a very small amount of space in your computer's memory. This entire book, which was written using word processing software, amounts to about one-and-a-half megabytes (1.5 million bytes) on my computer's hard drive. But what happens if you want to store a picture of your Aunt Sophie on your computer? A single color picture can require more digital 1s and 0s than is required for the text of this entire book.

If you want to get really fancy and store a digital video of Aunt Sophie blowing out candles on her birthday, you would require even more bytes. In fact, only about one or two seconds of Aunt Sophie in digital video would fit into the same amount of space required to store this book in computer memory.

The number of bytes required to store digital information is important to understand. As you start to put together your digital marketing promotions, the number of bytes you require will determine not only the cost of your promotion, but also its viability and effectiveness.

THE BASICS OF THE PERSONAL COMPUTER

Although computers come in many shapes and sizes — whether it is an Apple Macintosh (what I use), or an IBM or IBM-compatible PC — all personal computers are basically the same. In fact, even the most sophisticated supercomputer runs on basically the same structure as a desktop model. The following components of the personal computer are relevant to the field of digital marketing.

The CPU and processing speed: The Central Processing Unit (CPU) is the internal engine of a computer that does the actual computing and controls the flow of digital information (bits and bytes) from one place to another. In the beginning of the PC revolution in the early 1980s, CPUs were very slow compared to the processors in today's computers. But no one cared much because the software in those days only handled word processing and other text-based information. The number of bits and bytes was very small.

Today, however, computers are being asked to handle extremely complex calculations and move a tremendous number of 0s and 1s around, including pictures, graphics, and video. If your computer doesn't have a very fast processor, it can't handle these millions of bits and bytes. If it tried, your computer would either "crash," or run at a snail's pace. So when you're looking at buying a new computer for your marketing department, make sure it has a processor fast enough to handle video, sound, and full-color pictures. And more importantly, keep in mind that your customers may not have computers with high-speed processors. They may not be able to process a digital video or run a sophisticated multimedia program. Their computers may only be able to process text and perhaps a little bit of sound.

The speed of a processor is measured in megahertz (MHz) and indicates how quickly the processor can make calculations. Early PCs operated at about five MHz, while current computers operate at speeds of 75 MHz and higher. The more megahertz of processing speed you have in your computer, the faster you can run digital information. If you have a fast processor, for example, a digital video will run much smoother than on a computer with a slow processor.

Random Access Memory (RAM): When you are running your computer, you are using its Random Access Memory (RAM). This is the live, active memory of your computer. For example, if you are writing a letter on your computer, you are typing it into RAM. If the power goes off, and you haven't saved your letter to your hard drive or diskette, your letter will be lost and you'll have to retype it.

The RAM on your computer is measured in megabytes. In the early days of computers, one or two megabytes of RAM was sufficient (remember you were only writing up letters in those days). Today you need a lot more RAM to display pictures, audio, and video — at least eight, 16, or 32 megabytes of RAM. In the future, you will see computers that come with greater and greater amounts of standard RAM.

Like processing speed, understanding the economics of RAM is also important in developing an effective digital marketing program. If you create an elaborate Web site with all kinds of bells and whistles, you had better make sure your audience has enough RAM in their computers to run them. Time and time again, we have seen marketers — or at least their enthusiastic computer designers — create digital promotional material that is too sophisticated for their market. Ignore RAM at your peril!

Hard drives and storage: If you want to store information for a period of time on your computer, you store it on your hard drive, or on some other type of storage device such as a tape drive or a floppy disk. Most computer users store their digital bits and bytes on a hard drive. Back in the pioneer days, we used to think that a 20 megabyte hard drive was huge. Once again, you were only storing letters and recipes, so 20 megs was indeed sufficient.

Now you need much larger hard drives to store video and audio, perhaps a 400 megabyte or a 1,000 megabyte (gigabyte) hard drive. I was shocked recently when a gigabyte hard drive in my office ran out of storage space! I had never thought that I would ever use it all up. In the future, look for larger and larger storage devices to become common. As the price of storage falls, you will see computers with 100 gigabyte drives and larger become the norm.

Once again, an appreciation of the limitations of storage capacity is important in developing a digital marketing strategy. In the first place, you will probably need a greater amount of storage capacity in your office to handle all of the digital information you will accumulate. And second, you should be aware that most computers being used today are still equipped with very small hard drives. This will put a limit on the amount of information your audience can access and store on their computers.

Peripheral devices: These are pieces of hardware you attach to your computer in order to perform a specific function. If you want to scan pictures into your computer, you add a digital scanner or a digital still camera. If you want to add sounds to your computer, you attach a microphone or a sound mixing board. If you want to hear music on your computer, you add a sound board and speakers. If you want to create digital video, you add a digital video camera to your computer.

All these attachments are referred to as "peripherals." As time goes on, most new computers will come with many of these peripherals already installed. But bear in mind that most computer users in the world today are still using relatively unsophisticated computers with few, if any, peripherals. So if you plan to develop a digital marketing promotion with lots of digital video and elaborate sounds, your audience may not be equipped to enjoy them.

CD-ROM drives: The CD-ROM — which looks exactly like an audio compact disk (CD) — is one of the most important peripherals to understand in relation to digital marketing. The acronym ROM stands for Read Only Memory. This means you can read (or view) the information on the disk, but you can't change it. CD-ROMs have become very popular because they hold a large number of bytes — 640 megabytes to be exact. That's enough room to store two complete editions of an encyclopedia on one CD-ROM.

With the advent of CD-ROM it is now possible to store videos, sound, text and graphics, all on one, portable disk. As promotional tools, CD-ROMs allow you to put your entire catalogue on one disk, or to create stunning, full-video, electronic brochures. But if you are thinking about using a CD-ROM in your promotions, make sure the customers in your target market have CD-ROM drives on their computer. You must also make sure the software that runs the CD-ROM will operate properly on their computers. In many cases, recipients of promotional CD-ROMs can't run the disk because the software is too elaborate.

For some target markets, a CD-ROM may be the right solution. Computer industry studies say there are about 30 million computers worldwide that are capable of running a CD-ROM. About 15 million households in North America have CD-ROM drives. This number is expected to rise because most new computers are now sold with CD-ROM drives already installed.

The only drawback of CD-ROMs at this time is speed. It takes your computer many times longer to retrieve information from a CD-ROM than from a hard drive. This can cause a CD-ROM production to run slowly, especially if there are a lot of graphics and video images to download.

In the next few years, you will see the emergence of the next generation of CD-ROMs, called Digital Video Disk (DVD). The new DVD format will have much greater storage capacity, with some projections seeing the capacity reaching 17 gigabytes on one disk by the end of the century. The increased capacity of CD-ROMs is sure to fuel continued use of this technology for marketing purposes.

MODEMS AND BANDWIDTH

A modem (the word stands for Modulator/Demodulator) is used to transmit digital information from one computer to another over regular telephone lines. When you want to send a computer file to another computer across town, your modem takes your bytes and turns (modulates) them into sounds. These sounds are transmitted over the telephone lines and picked up by a modem at the other end. The receiving modem turns the sounds back into bytes (demodulates) and passes them on to the receiving computer. The reason this modulating/demodulating process is necessary is because regular telephone lines are not able to transport digital information directly; they are designed to send sound only.

How fast a modem can send and receive bytes is called its "Baud Rate," and the speed is calculated in bits per second (bps). Back in the days of yore, a modem with a baud rate of 1,200 bits per second (bps) was sufficient. But now we are seeing modems with speeds of 14,400 bps (14.4), 28,800 (28.8) and beyond. At present, the standard speed of most modems is 14,400 bps, although the 28,800 bps models are quickly becoming the norm.

When you are developing your digital marketing strategy, you must consider the speed of the modems used by your audience. If most of your customers and prospects are still using 14.4 modems, you shouldn't put a giant digital video on your Web site that will take them two hours to download. The most common mistake we see is a Web site with a really large color graphic on its first page. A visitor to the site, using a 14.4 modem, has to wait about three or four minutes for the graphic to appear on his screen. Most visitors, bored to tears, will probably move on to another site before the graphic appears, and will avoid the site in the future.

The issue of modem speeds is known in the digital industry as the "bandwidth" problem. As digital promotions become richer in color graphics and text, the delivery system has become less and less capable of delivering them. In many cases, it is like trying to use a dirt road to move the rush hour traffic of a major city. There are huge tie-ups and everything moves at a glacial pace. Later on in this chapter, I'll discuss some of the ways that cable companies, telephone utilities, and other parties are working to solve this bandwidth problem.

Once again, you must assess the bandwidth capacity of your audience when you are developing your digital marketing strategy. Remember that most people who use modems are still using 2,400 and 14.4 bps versions. They may not be ready for your 2.2 gigabyte digital marketing extravaganza.

SOFTWARE YOU NEED TO UNDERSTAND

If you want to get involved in digital marketing, you need to understand the fundamentals of the basic software programs. From my experience, I've found that most people know one or two applications, but think that programs such as spreadsheets and databases are mysterious netherworlds.

Word processing (WP): Most of us are familiar with word processing for writing letters and doing basic layout for newsletters and brochures. Two of the more popular word processing programs are *Microsoft Word* and *WordPerfect*.

Spreadsheets (SS): You use a spreadsheet to make calculations. On a grid, you enter numbers in a column and then use formulas to add them together. For example, you may want to calculate how much to charge for a product. You would put all your costs into the spreadsheet, which would then automatically calculate how much your wholesale and retail prices should be. You can play around with the numbers, and create "what if?" scenarios.

Databases (DB): Think of a database as a large filing cabinet. You can put almost anything into this filing cabinet including names, addresses, pictures, and sounds. You can then sort this information in a host of different ways. You can, for example, find out which of your customers in Pittsburgh have the first name Bob. Or which customers in your store spend more than $1,000 a year. If you are going to do digital marketing, you must learn how to use a database, and then set up a database of your customers.

Graphic design software: These software applications, such as *Pagemaker*, *QuarkXpress,* and *Photoshop*, are used for advanced graphic design. Although you do not need to be an expert at using these programs to do digital marketing, you should familiarize yourself with their basic features. *Pagemaker* and *QuarkXpress* are used for layout, and *Photoshop* is used to manipulate pictures and graphics. You would use *Pagemaker* to design your newsletter or your annual report. You would use *Photoshop* to change the color in a picture.

Multimedia software: You use multimedia software, such as *MacroMind Director*, *Microsoft PowerPoint* or *Adobe Premier*, to create presentations with text, video, graphics, sound, and pictures. They can be used to create marketing presentations on your laptop, or multimedia shows that can be downloaded over the Internet. Some of these programs are easier to use than others. New software programs will make it easier and easier for just about anyone to create multimedia presentations.

If you learn the basics of these programs, or at least understand what they are used for, you can add them to your digital marketing strategy if appropriate. I would suggest emphatically that you learn more about databases if your knowledge about them is limited.

THE BASICS OF ONLINE TECHNOLOGY

The Internet: Perhaps no single digital media has attracted as much attention from marketers as the Internet. Its explosive growth over the past few years has created a firestorm of interest from marketers who want to use it to sell products and services.

The Internet has its origins in the 1960s when the Department of Defense in the United States wanted to build a communications network that would be invulnerable to a nuclear attack. They wanted to have a way to send digital information to computers all over the world, over many different routes, even if part of the network had been destroyed.

To achieve this goal, the Advanced Research and Projects Agency (ARPA) created a computer protocol called TCP/IP (Transmission Control Protocol/Internet Protocol) and built a network called ARPANET. Over the years, the network grew to include universities, government departments, and large corporations. Around 1990, smaller businesses and individuals began to connect to the system, which by that time had become known as the Internet. It wasn't until the invention of the World Wide Web in 1993 that the Internet became a household word.

From a marketing perspective, it is important to realize how the Internet works, not just the World Wide Web. That's because there are many opportunities for marketing other than just setting up a Web site. The Internet should be seen as a transmission system. You don't have to limit your strategic thinking to the Web only.

It's important to understand how the TCP/IP protocol works. Information sent over the Internet is packaged or divided into sections called *packets*. The packets are put into envelopes based on the Transmission Control Protocol, and the Internet Protocol labels the envelope with the address of the destination computer. All digital information sent over the Internet must follow this TCP/IP protocol.

Every computer that is connected to the Internet has an Internet address. There are two types of addresses: a numeric *IP Address* such as 121.154.6.44, or a *domain name* such as biginc.on.ca. The domain name system is more commonly used than the numeric IP system. This is especially true in marketing situations because a name is much easier to remember than a number. When an e-mail message is sent over the Internet, the computers that direct the Internet traffic (called routers) know where the computer with a particular domain name is located. The message moves from one router to another until it reaches the computer with the right domain or IP address.

Most major companies have registered their domain names such as IBM.com, Coke.com, or McDonalds.com. Some consumer products companies have also registered domain names for their products, or for words that allude to their products, such as kleenex.com, or headache.com.

Registering your domain name: If you're thinking about marketing using the Internet, you should register your domain name immediately. You want to secure a domain name appropriate for your company before someone else takes it. We have a few clients who were unable to get the domain name they wanted because someone else had already registered it. They wished they had registered their domain name much sooner instead of waiting.

If you wish to register your domain name for marketing, you will probably want to register one that ends with .com. This stands for "commercial." There are other domain extensions such as .net (for Internet service providers) or .edu (for educational institutions). To register your domain name, first conduct a search to see if the one you want is taken. This can be done using the World Wide Web, or through your Internet provider. If the name you want is available, submit your application to Network Solutions, the agency that approves domain name applications. There is usually a small fee for registering the name, and an annual fee for keeping it.

For example, Veronica Byte at Walrus Design was lucky enough to get the domain name walrus.com. That means that her e-mail address is veronica@walrus.com. The address of her Web site is www.walrus.com. By using this domain name, it is much easier for people to remember her e-mail address and the location of her Web site.

If the commercial domain (.com) name you want is already taken, your second option is to get a geographical domain name. If some other company had already taken the walrus.com, Veronica could have applied for a domain name such as walrus.on.ca, which means that her company is located in Ontario, Canada (on.ca). Veronica's other option would be to get a domain name that represents her Web site such as retailworld.com. She could, in fact, register both walrus.com, and retailworld.com.

My best advice about domain names is to act immediately. Thousands of applications are submitted to Network Solutions every day. If you wait, you will probably lose out on getting the domain name you want. *Even if you aren't ready to do marketing on the Internet, it is still wise to secure the domain name you want right now.*

THE MANY FACES OF THE INTERNET

Because the World Wide Web has popularized the Internet, many people have the impression that the Web is the Internet. That is not the case. In addition to the World Wide Web, the Internet is used for many applications. Here is a brief description of each of these applications.

E-mail: This is the most common application of the Internet. You can send and receive messages from anyone in the world who has an e-mail address. You can also attach computer files, such as a word processing document or a multimedia application, to an e-mail message. I believe that e-mail will become the most powerful digital marketing tool once everyone has an e-mail address. In a later chapter, we will discuss some of the interesting marketing strategies you can devise using e-mail.

Newsgroups: If you want to chat with other people on the Internet you turn to the newsgroups, which are electronic discussion groups on the section of the Internet known as Usenet. Each newsgroup is dedicated to a specific topic such as football or knitting. You can read the messages in a newsgroup, and respond with your own messages. Using newsgroups for marketing purposes is a good idea, but it has to be done in the proper manner. I will discuss newsgroup marketing later in more detail.

File Transfer Protocol (FTP): This is a method of transferring files from one computer to another. You give people the address of your FTP site and they can go there and pick up that file. When you visit a FTP site, all you see is a list of files; there are no graphics and text describing the files. Although an FTP site is not normally considered in a marketing strategy, you may set one up to provide ready access to computer files, especially if you are a software company or a provider of other digital information.

Your own custom Internet platform: When you use the Internet, you have the choice of using any of the standard Internet platforms, as long as you have the right software. For the World Wide Web, you use a browser such as *Mosaic* or *Netscape*. For e-mail, you might use a program called *Eudora*. For newsgroups, you might use *NetNews*, and for FTP, you might use a program called *Fetch*.

As time goes on, other platforms will emerge for the Internet, which may or may not have marketing applications. In fact, this is where the great opportunity lies: If you develop a strategy for digital marketing, you may decide you want to develop your own platform that runs on the Internet. You may decide that you want to create a platform that links you and your customers, over the Internet, in a unique fashion.

For example, if you run a business supplies store, you might want to create a customized software program that allows your customers to order products using their computer. This software would be unique to your company and it would also run over the Internet. Once again, I emphasize, you don't have to limit your thinking to the World Wide Web; that might be completely the wrong strategy.

If you took a look at your market and found out only 25 percent of your customers use the World Wide Web, your Web site strategy would leave out 75 percent of your other customers. You might decide you want to have an online system that can be accessed through the Internet and through regular telephone lines for those customers who have a modem, but who don't have an Internet account. As well, you may wish to allow your customers without a modem to access your online ordering system over the telephone. After all, every business customer has a telephone.

So remember, you don't have to limit your strategic thinking to the World Wide Web. You can use all the other tools on the Internet, or create your own Internet platform. As long as it operates under the standard TCP/IP protocol, you can use any platform on the Internet. But first you have to take a look at your audience to see what digital tools they use to communicate. If they are all using the World Wide Web, then a Web site makes the most sense. If most of your customers have modems, but they're not hooked up to an Internet service provider (ISP), you might want to create a system that runs over regular telephone lines such as a private BBS. We will discuss this in more detail in Chapter 8.

COMPUTER BULLETIN BOARD SERVICES (BBS)

The online revolution began with the use of bulletin board services, better known as BBSs. Back in the early 1980s, people all over the world set up BBS systems in their offices and homes. They attached a number of modems to their computer, installed BBS software, and gave out the modem telephone number of their BBS. Other people connected their computer to the BBS by using their modem. Once online, they could send and receive messages from other users.

These BBS systems grew dramatically. Some BBS administrators had hundreds of modems connected to their systems, which allowed hundreds of people to connect to their system at one time. Some of the BBS systems were based on single topics such as science fiction, or Microsoft software, while other BBS systems were general in subject matter.

Today, anyone can set up a BBS. All you need is a computer, a few modems, and BBS software. In the "old" days, a BBS was text only. Now BBS systems can be rich in graphics and functionality. When the World Wide Web exploded onto the scene in 1994, many people predicted the death of the BBS. This is the farthest from the truth. I believe BBS systems will become even more popular as the hype over the World Wide Web begins to wear thin.

In the last two years, my company has set up about 12 different BBS systems. Our clients were looking for an online system that would allow their customers to connect with them electronically, but they realized most of their customers were not on the Internet. The BBS system gives their customers a way to get online without an Internet account. As well, the BBS can be available through regular telephone lines and through the Internet simultaneously — a definite advantage over the World Wide Web.

Once again, it all depends on your target market. If all your customers are on the Internet, then a Web site is the answer. If your audience has computers, but only a handful are on the Internet, you might choose the BBS route. If your audience doesn't use computers at all, then you have to look at other digital tools such as smart cards, interactive voice-response systems, or fax-on-demand systems. I will discuss all the other digital tools, and explain their marketing applications, in Chapter 8.

THE BATTLE FOR BANDWIDTH

If there is one term that has been used to death, it is the "Information Superhighway." But what does it actually mean? For starters, the Internet is not the Information Superhighway. Right now the Internet is just too slow for most users, especially those using 14.4 and 28.8 kbps modems. There just isn't enough bandwidth on the Internet right now to call it a "superhighway."

When people talk about the Information Superhighway, they're really dreaming about the future when everyone has a high-speed connection to the Internet coming right into their television set. When that happens, all the couch potatoes — who don't want to get up and sit behind a computer — will be able to surf the Net and buy pizza and lottery tickets online.

The people who want to make PotatoNet possible are the telephone and cable companies. They are vying to bring high-speed digital connections into your home. The cable companies seem to have the lead right now because most homes already have a coaxial cable installed. (Coaxial cable can transport many more bits per second than regular telephone lines.) Rogers Cable in Toronto, for example, is set to introduce The Wave, which will allow you to access the Internet at speeds of up to 500,000 bits per second. That's about 16 times faster than is possible with an 28.8 kbps modem. This makes it possible to access and download large digital video files in a split second instead of minutes or hours. It's a very exciting development.

The telephone companies, on the other hand, have their own plans. For years, they have been patiently laying fiber optic cables — which can transport even more bits per second than coaxial cable — right next to your house. Unfortunately for the telcos, the cost of running the fiber optic cable that extra 50 feet into your house will be extremely high. They're working on a way to use digital compression in order to make your regular telephone lines send and receive more bits than it is currently capable of doing. (Compression takes digital files and makes them smaller, which in turn makes them faster to transmit.)

My bet is the cable companies will win the war to bring you PotatoNet. You'll then be able to surf the Internet using your channel changer, and whole new online standards will emerge. For example, regular television shows will have interactive content. While watching a commercial, you'll be able to click on an icon and get more information about a product by going to its Web site. You will be able to order products from a local store directly from your TV. I believe the widespread use of cable modems will cause an explosion in online marketing that will make the current commercial frenzy on the Internet look like a church bazaar.

THE MULTIMEDIA REVOLUTION

As we've seen, information stored on computers is digital in nature, made up of 1s and 0s. During the past ten years, more and more communication devices have become digital in nature — including audio compact disks (CDs), digital cellular telephones, and computer games. In 1995, we witnessed the release of *Toy Story*, the first, all-digital feature-length movie.

As time goes on, virtually every communications medium will be converted to a digital format. Telephone lines and cable will become digital. Radio will be digital. Your VCR will soon become a digital device. This is what has become known as the Digital or Multimedia Revolution, and before you start planning your digital marketing strategy, make sure that you understand what this revolution is all about.

What exactly does the term "multimedia" mean? I believe that it has three primary characteristics:

1. It's the ability to combine many different media such as text, pictures, sounds, and video in one presentation.
2. Users can interact with a multimedia presentation, either by choosing the information they want to see, or by adding input of their own.
3. All the information in a multimedia presentation is stored in a digital format.

One other way people describe the multimedia revolution is by applying the term "convergence." This usually refers to the merging of communications media companies such as cable companies, telephone utilities, television networks, and movie production companies. But convergence also means the blending of different media together into one entity. For example, it won't be long before your television set, computer, telephone, and home security system are all linked together into one digital device.

GET ACQUAINTED WITH THE DIGITAL WORLD

If you are interested in digital marketing, you should get hands-on experience using digital and online technology. Surf the Internet and find out what your competitors are up to. Try out CD-ROMs. Learn how to create a database and build a spreadsheet. Try out a digital still camera or a digital video camera. Get an e-mail address and register your domain name. From this experience, you'll be able to work more comfortably within the digital marketing environment, and you'll develop a more effective digital marketing strategy.

You are now ready to begin developing your own digital marketing strategy by reading Section Two.

SECTION TWO

PLANNING YOUR DIGITAL MARKETING STRATEGY

CHAPTER 5

CREATE YOUR DIGITAL VISION

He knew this was among the alternatives today, a fact along lines of the future radiating from this position in time-space. The imperfect vision haunted him... His entire future was becoming like a river hurtling toward a chasm — the violent nexus beyond which all was fog and clouds.

Dune
Frank Herbert, 1965

When you can imagine many possible futures ahead of you, it's hard to decide which one you want to realize. That's what happens to Paul, the hero of Frank Herbert's novel, *Dune*. By eating the spice melange, a precious commodity found only on the planet Arrakis, Paul acquires the prophetic power to see into the future, and every time he acts, the future he sees is changed. He cannot decide which vision of the future he wishes to achieve.

Looking into the future is your first task in setting out a strategic digital marketing initiative. You need to establish your business objectives and decide how you can use digital technology to realize them. I call this your Digital Vision and I emphasize that the sole purpose for using digital technology is to help you achieve your business objectives. All too often, companies get lost in the technology and forget their real business goals. Ask yourself: "Is it our goal to build a Web site or put in a corporate-wide information system?" or "Is it our goal to increase sales revenue and profits?" "Is it our goal to put in an interactive voice-response system or is it to improve customer service?" As you can see, when you look first at your business objectives, you start thinking more strategically about digital technology. You start to ask yourself: "What are we really trying to achieve, anyway?" Keep this question in mind while you're developing your Digital Vision. Technology should be the servant of your business objectives, not the master.

Your Digital Vision may be a personal one, or it may be a vision for your company or your department. It all depends, of course, on your situation. If you're running your own business, you may wish to set objectives for your company over the next five to ten years. If you're running a marketing department of a large corporation, your objectives may be short term, perhaps over the next 12 months. To help you develop your Digital Vision, I will look at possible goals that are short term (over the next 12 months), medium term (one to three years) and long term (three to five years).

LONG-TERM DIGITAL GOALS

Begin by creating a long-term vision. Think about what your company will look like in the next five years. What products and services will you sell? Who will be your customers? Who will work for your company? How will digital technology be used to run your company? Within this framework, think about creative ideas that will tie all your promotional efforts together. This is the idea that will draw people to your Digital Domain. It may also be the way in which your company becomes the digital leader in your industry.

Here's an example. Let's say you're in the trucking business. As we learned from Theodore Levitt and his theory of marketing myopia, you're actually in the transportation business, not just the trucking business. I would like to take this one step further. You are not only in the business of moving things from A to B, you are also in the business of moving bits and bytes. For example, you might take your knowledge of the trucking and transportation business and create an information system for your whole industry. Here's one possible scenario I will call ShipNet.

ShipNet: An industry-wide information system: As a transportation company, you create an online service to help companies move their shipments across North America in the most efficient manner possible. Called ShipNet, the service gives customers the ability to create their own transportation system. Using their computer hooked to your online service via modem, they choose from a variety of different shipping methods — air, sea, truck, or container — and from different pricing and delivery speed options.

The software matches up the shipper's request with the various transportation companies and factors in their routes and delivery times. As you can see, the customer actually creates his own transportation company by selecting the most suitable mix of transportation services.

The advantages of developing ShipNet go beyond the profits you make selling the service to customers; you also sell the service to your competitors. Other trucking and transportation companies participate in ShipNet because it brings them a steady stream of business. As well, ShipNet allows competing companies to exchange shipments with each other in the most efficient and mutually beneficial way possible.

If you envision this idea, or one similar to it, and make its implementation a long-term goal, you will become the most profitable and powerful player in the industry. Like American Airlines and its Sabre system, you will receive a commission on every shipment made through ShipNet. You might decide running a trucking company is a waste of time, and just run ShipNet. (In fact, Knight-Ridder Inc. offers a modest version of ShipNet called Trans/Rates which provides online access to the rates and schedules of shipping companies.)

Setting up a system like ShipNet not only requires a long-term vision; it also requires a major commitment of resources. But where is your trucking company going to be five years from now anyway? Do you want to be sending out trucks that get rusty and need regular maintenance, or will you be gathering electronic commissions on the Information Highway?

BeautyWare: Your own software and info-products: If you are a major producer of cosmetics, your long-term vision might be to create an information service called BeautyWare. Using your knowledge of the beauty industry, you create software and information products to help people look more beautiful and stay healthier. These information products are distributed using a variety of digital devices including CD-ROM and the World Wide Web. For example, you produce a BeautyWare CD-ROM that covers every facet of the beauty business — exercise, nutrition, cosmetics, skin care, and stress management. The CD-ROM is given away as a promotion for your company, or better yet, sold at cosmetic counters. In addition, you create software that allows cosmeticians to choose the best cosmetics for their clients. This software uses a digital camera to take a picture of the client's face, which is edited onscreen to show different ideas for hairstyles and makeup application. Because the software is sponsored by a major cosmetics company, it gains wide acceptance by both cosmeticians and the public.

The key point is to make it your goal to "informationalize" your business. Use your knowledge to create information products and services.

The FishMinder: Smart products and services: Your long-term vision could include developing "smart" products and services. This means adding digital and online capabilities to your existing products and services.

Let's say you're in the pet store business. You team up with a supplier of tropical fish tanks and accessories. You develop a smart tropical fish tank, and a service called the FishMinder to monitor your customers' fish. The fish tank has built-in sensors and controls that allow you to remotely monitor and adjust the tank's water temperature, nitrogen levels, and other factors. FishMinder includes a digital camera that keeps track of the fish and their health. If the tank requires cleaning or the fish need attention, you call the customer or send an e-mail message with a report on the problem. Each time you communicate with your customer, you create an opportunity to sell additional services and tropical fish products.

The smart fish tank and the FishMinder service might seem far-fetched, but the principle is sound. Just about any product and service can be turned into a smart one. A car manufacturer can create a vehicle with a built-in cellular modem that monitors the car's condition. The car owner receives regular e-mail messages detailing the car's condition along with maintenance recommendations. An electronics manufacturer might create a portable music player that allows you to download and play complete music tracks. You simply attach the device to your computer, visit the appropriate music company Web site, download the music, and transfer it to the portable device.

These are just some ideas to help you envision your long-term future. The development of industry-wide information systems or smart products might take many years of work and a large outlay of capital, but if you begin the process now, and give yourself time, you can achieve virtually any goal in the digital age.

MEDIUM-TERM DIGITAL GOALS

Although the complete integration of digital technology into your organization will probably take five years, there are many goals that can be achieved over the medium term. Your vision for one to three years may include the following elements:

New digital markets: Digital and online technology can help you reach markets that were unavailable to you before the advent of the Internet. You're no longer restricted to your local marketplace by the cost of long-distance telephone calls, or the expense of mass-media advertising. You can place your Digital Domain on the Internet, and attract interested parties from anywhere in the world.

With technology such as InternetPhone (which allows for international calls on the Internet), you can work with someone in Asia with the same ease as dealing with someone across town.

Digital economies of scale: Low-cost access to a global market allows you to create very specialized products and services not viable within your local market. For example, you might want to sell a line of high-end pruning shears for Japanese bonsai trees. If you tried to sell these shears in your own country, you might only find 100 bonsai enthusiasts willing to pay for premium pruning paraphernalia — certainly not enough customers to sustain a business. But around the world there could be more than 30,000 people who are desperate for a better way to prune their bonsai. By tapping into electronic discussion groups on the Internet that pertain to bonsai trees (you can create them if they don't exist), you can build a global awareness of your Bonsai Pruning Shears at a very low cost. You can ship the shears directly to the customer by overnight courier. Within this larger global market, you can reach the economies of scale necessary to make almost any specialized product or service viable.

Point-to-point digital markets: Digital technology allows you to develop products and services sold exclusively to customers in a single geographical area, or within a single organization, somewhere else in the world. For example, your local climate might be ideally suited to grow an exotic herb coveted by people who live in Tanzania, or you might be the most appropriate person to create specialized software products prized by school teachers in Istanbul. Using the communications tools of the Internet, and online access to market research databases, you can conceivably source thousands of niche markets around the world.

New digital assets: Over the next three years, your company might aim to create new digital and information assets that will increase the value of your organization. These digital assets can include the following:

A. Your customer database: Your digital marketing strategy must focus on how to expand and enhance the richness of this database. As it becomes larger and more useful, it will help you increase your sales and, if appropriate, it can become an asset you sell or rent to other organizations.

B. Other digital databases: In addition to a customer database, you should constantly expand the wealth of useful information your company has stored in a digital format. Depending on your line of business, this storehouse of knowledge might include market research findings, technology development information, product specifications, and professional reports. This information could be repackaged and sold online or through other digital media such as a fax-on-demand system or a CD-ROM.

Here are a few ideas on how these digital databases can be used:

> **LogoNet:** In addition to text, your information database might include digital assets in the form of pictures, video, and sound. For example, in my marketing communications business, we've considered developing LogoNet. We are always converting print-based logos into a digital format when we produce a Web site or a BBS network, and we now have about 100 corporate logos in a digital format. If we made it our vision to digitize the logos of all the major corporations in North America, we would have a very valuable asset. We could create an online service (LogoNet) which provides digital logos to graphic designers. Instead of having to digitize the logo themselves, they could simply download it from LogoNet.
>
> **PhotoNet:** If you're a photographer, you could create a database of all your photographs in a digital format. Your digital photographs could be downloaded directly from a Web site (for a fee) and used by graphic designers anywhere in the world. To make this database more valuable, and to compete against the large photo service bureaus, a small

photography company would be wise to specialize in a particular type of photography, or in a particular subject matter. This will make it easier to position the service in the minds of potential customers.

EatNet: If you publish a magazine about restaurants, you might consider creating a database of all the restaurants in the world (or at least in your own city). The more information you put into this database about each restaurant (menus, interviews with chefs, digital videos of happy diners, or pictures of each food item), the more valuable it will be. People will seek out this database because it contains *all* the restaurants, and *all* the information you want about each restaurant. Once again, this database could be placed online or distributed by CD-ROM, fax-on-demand, or even by telephone.

New digital partnerships: Digital technology allows you to operate a worldwide organization that runs from a single computer. Your medium-term goal could be to create a virtual company that brings together experts from the four corners of the globe. For example, you might be a designer/builder of smart homes. With your own online network, you could bring together an architect from the British Virgin Islands, a wiring expert from Calcutta, an interior designer from England, and a computer consultant from Silicon Valley. As a team, you could design the most advanced smart homes in the world.

Or you could be a publisher of educational text books. You could bring together content from teachers in every country, and create the most comprehensive and varied textbooks (or multimedia CD-ROM learning tools) ever used by students.

Exploit latent digital capabilities: As your company has grown, you have developed a lot of expertise in producing your products or in providing your services. In the course of providing your core product/service, you may have also developed innovative ways to handle your accounting, warehouse management, human resources administration, or marketing and promotional efforts. The expertise you've developed in these areas may contain "latent digital capabilities" you may wish to exploit.

For example, you may have created an innovative software program to handle your company's flexible benefits program. You might consider taking that proprietary software program and selling it to other companies. Or you might have invented a way to manage your warehouse distribution in a more efficient manner using bar code scanners, and robot conveyance machines. You might turn around and market this technology and expertise to other companies.

So take a close look at your company's capabilities. Have you invented a way of doing things that could be turned into its own product and service? If so, it could spawn a new and profitable company.

The end of intermediaries: If a middleman asks you "For whom does the digital bell toll?" tell him "It tolls for thee." The digital age spells the end of the traditional middleman. As a producer of a product or service, you no longer need as much help from retailers, wholesalers, agents, and brokers, along with mass-media intermediaries such as magazines, radio stations, and outdoor ad companies. In the digital age, you communicate directly with the customer. And the customer is able to buy products and services directly from you. Of course, you may still need retailers to sell your products, and you may still need to advertise in a newspaper, but digital distribution channels give you much greater bargaining power with every intermediary you encounter. My advice is to take a look at all your intermediary distribution and promotional channels, and develop a vision for eliminating as many of them as possible in the next three years.

SHORT-TERM DIGITAL GOALS

Although you should begin with a long-term Digital Vision, you may have pressing issues that need to be addressed over the short term.

You may have a product in need of promotion, or inventory languishing in your warehouse. You may have a new competitor breathing down your neck, or an advertising program that's going nowhere. Used properly, digital technology may be able to help you immediately. Here are some short-term scenarios:

Promote a new product or service: Let's say you're launching your new premium Bonsai Pruning Shears and you want to reach your worldwide market of bonsai lovers. You create a Web site about the product and list the site with all the major Internet search engines. If someone is looking for information about bonsai trees on the Internet, they first go to a search engine and enter "bonsai trees." They see a list like this one gathered by the Excite search engine:

American Bonsai Society

Bonsai Illustrated explanations of some bonsai terms

Bonsai Mailing List Discussion of the art and craft of Bonsai and related art forms

FAQ Bonsai

Premium Bonsai Pruning Shears Launched!

Bonsai Resource Page

Internet Bonsai Club

The Gainesville, FL, Bonsai Society

Bonsai in Britain — The Federation of British Bonsai Societies (FOBBS) and the UK

National Bonsai Collection. Some bonsai basics for beginners.

Bonsai icons

Bonsai Online Ezine devoted to bonsai lovers

Bonsai Styling & Advice Corner. Several trees with typical problems. Comments from online club members. Your comments welcome.

The Ikenobo Ikebana Society of South Florida

The Morikami Museum and Japanese Gardens

The home page for Bonsai Societies of Florida

Bonsai Clubs in the United States and Canada — listing of bonsai clubs in the United States and Canada, including contact information, meeting places, and club activities.

To access your site, the potential customer clicks on Premium Bonsai Pruning Shears Launched! If they like what they see, the customer can order the shears by sending you an e-mail message or by filling out an online order form.

But this is just the beginning. You go to each of these Web sites and become involved with the Internet bonsai community which, incidentally, is enormous. You contribute an article on "Why You Need Special Shears to Trim a Bonsai" and post it with Bonsai Online and with other bonsai sites. You also ask them to create direct links from their sites to your site. You also use the Internet to gather lists of organizations that will be useful in helping you get the word out about your product. You get the list from the Bonsai Clubs in the United States and Canada site and create a database. You send out e-mail and fax messages to the people in the database announcing the launch of your product.

To give you an idea of the marketing value of these lists found on the Internet, here are three entries, among the 500 I found in the Bonsai Club list after only one minute of searching:

CALIFORNIA — Arcadia
Santa Anita Bonsai Society. Meets at 301 N. Baldwin Ave., Arcadia, second Saturday of each month except July, August, and December, 7:30 p.m. Gene Cannon, 24303 Woolsey Canyon Rd. #2, Canoga Park, CA 91304, (818) 9995486 or Jim Barrett, (818) 4454529.

CALIFORNIA — Arcadia
Shohin Bonsai Society. Meets at Los Angeles Arboretum, 301 N. Baldwin Ave., Arcadia, second Wednesday, except July and August, 7:30 PM. Marty Hagbery, (818) 3328381, or Edith Izant, 1021 Sierra Vista Dr., La Habra, CA 90631, (310) 6913450. Bonsai 10" and under. Annual show second weekend in April. Meetings have guest speakers and frequent workshops.

CALIFORNIA — Arcata
Humboldt Bonsai Society. Meets at homes of members at varied dates. Karen Haas, PO Box 816, Trinidad, CA 95570, (707) 6770636. Membership consists of individuals residing in several cities in the Humboldt Bay area.

The idea is to become immersed in the Internet bonsai community. You put together an Internet promotion that costs about the same as one small ad in a bonsai magazine. You roll out the promotion in a matter of days — even hours, for that matter. This is not to say you wouldn't use traditional promotional media and methods to introduce your bonsai shears, but digital technology can make the difference, especially if your budget is limited or time is short.

Improve customer service: You can use digital and online technology to improve the quality of your customer service, such as:

A. Private online network: As the owner of a financial services consulting company, you might want to improve customer service over the next 12 months. You want to speed up the process of administering accounts, while having more time to work face-to-face with your best customers. To do this, you create your own private online network (BBS) which allows your customers to look up the status of their account and to request changes. You post electronic forms for customers to download to their computer, fill out on screen, and then upload back to you. Instead of printing your newsletter and mailing it out, you post the same information to the BBS electronically.

By setting up your own online network, instead of simply creating a Web site, you provide a much higher level of perceived value to your customer. (In Chapter 8 — Choose Your Digital Tools — I will look at the difference between a BBS and a Web site.) The software for the network is provided on disk, and mailed out in an attractive installation package. The software displays your logo on the customer's screen every time they log in. The customer is able to communicate directly with their account executive by e-mail.

Canada Trust was the first major financial institution in Canada to introduce a service similar to this one. Now bank, trust company, and life insurance company customers can connect online to check account balances and pay bills electronically.

B. Fax-on-demand: In addition to a private online network, you could use a variety of other digital tools to improve customer service such as a fax-on-demand system. For example, a software company could place all its 2,000 technical documents on a fax system. You provide your customers with a booklet that contains a list of these documents and a code for each one. When the customer needs one or several of these documents, he dials up the system and enters the code or codes and his fax number. The documents are faxed to him automatically in minutes. Hewlett-Packard has used a fax-on-demand system for many years to provide technical specification sheets to its dealers around the world. (I will explain in detail the benefits of a fax-on-demand system in Chapter 8.)

C. Ident-a-call system: You can set up an inbound telemarketing center on your PC that rivals even the largest telemarketing company. When a call comes in, the system displays the telephone number of the caller, and links it to your database. When you pick up the telephone, your database automatically displays the current record you have about that person. You answer, "Hello Mr. Smith. Thank you for calling us." You are ready to help the customer faster because you already have the information you need in front of you. Many hotels have implemented this type of system for their front desk and room service staff. When you call down to the front desk, the concierge answers you by name. It may be a small point, but it's something a lot of hotel guests remember.

D. Follow-up database marketing: By using a database to track purchases, you can improve customer service and increase sales in the short term. Let's say you're an appliance retailer. Six months after a purchase, you call the customer to see how satisfied he is with his new microwave or stove. You tell him it's your policy to have a technician visit customers six months after a purchase to make sure the appliance is functioning properly.

When the technician arrives at the customer's house, he checks out the purchased product and makes any adjustments required. He also offers to check out the other appliances in the house. He finds the refrigerator is leaking freon and should be repaired, the coffee maker is broken, and the toaster oven is ten years old. Back in the service truck, the technician enters this information into a handheld personal digital assistant (PDA) and uploads it to the customer database by wireless modem. The sales department opens up the file and puts together a package about special deals on refrigerators, coffee makers, and toaster ovens. This flyer is sent out to the customer by e-mail, regular mail, or fax. A salesperson also calls the customer and tells him about the special promotions related to the products he needs.

Unload excess inventory: If you're a wholesaler or retailer who is chronically afflicted with excess inventory, you might find relief by setting up an online auction that operates on the reverse auction format. Instead of bidding higher and higher for an item, a reverse auction starts at a high price. The price drops until someone commits to buying the inventory. Prior to each auction, you list the products on the block for a few days and indicate the time of the auction. At the appointed time, potential buyers log on and watch the price fall. When the price is right, the buyer clicks a button on the screen, and the countdown stops. The successful bidder fills out an online form and gives you his credit card number and you ship the product to him by express. The Reverse Online Auction can be used for almost any product, such as last-minute vacations and airline tickets. (There is one company called The Internet Auction currently using this form of auction.)

Increase market awareness: Increasing awareness of your product or service might be one of your goals over the next year. You could put a Web site on the Internet, but you know that most of your customers are about 55 to 60 years old and they don't use the Internet. However, all use the telephone. You could use new calling card technology to raise awareness of your products, and even increase immediate sales of your product.

Calling card promotion: Let's say you are trying to sell the Gazelle 9000, a brand-new $60,000 high-end automobile. You create a credit card-size calling card with your logo and a picture of the new car. Each card has a unique personal identification number (PIN). You mail out the card, along with some promotional literature, to 20,000 owners of cars in the $60,000 range who bought their car three years ago (believe me, you can get such a list). The accompanying letter explains the card can be used to make 15 minutes of long-distance calls to anywhere in North America.

When the person comes to use the card, he is greeted by a voice that says, "Thank you for calling the Gazelle 9000 Calling Card Hotline. Before we activate your free 15 minutes, we would like to explain some of the features of the Gazelle 9000." The short advertisement is followed by a number of prompts. "If you would like us to stop by your house or office for a test drive, press 1. If you would like to speak with one of our representatives, press 2. If you would like the location of the nearest Gazelle 9000 dealership, enter your postal code or zip code now." Following the interactive portion, the card is then activated and the caller can place his call. Keep in mind that you don't even need to send out the card; you could simply print out the letters with unique PIN numbers. However, the calling card itself is more portable and durable; it is also a collector's item.

Other short-term goals: There are many other short-term goals that can be achieved using digital technology. To create more effective sales presentations, you can use laptop computers, CD-ROMs, and multimedia software. To lower marketing costs, you can use digital promotions instead of traditional mass-media advertising. To lower traveling expenses, you can use video-conferencing and e-mail. The list goes on.

HOLD A DIGITAL STRATEGY SESSION

I recommend you take one or two days to develop your Digital Vision. Bring together everyone in your company who has expertise or interest in this subject. Discuss the business goals you have for your organization, and then work on developing a clear vision for the future. Don't move on to the next stage and start playing with the technology until you know exactly what you're trying to achieve.

In the next chapter, I will look at the next step in the process, researching your digital market.

CHAPTER 6

RESEARCH YOUR DIGITAL MARKET

The throbbing grew louder, more insistent. Presently the man-apes began to move forward, like sleepwalkers, toward the source of that compulsive sound. Sometimes they took little dancing steps, as their blood responded to rhythms that their descendants would not create for ages yet. Totally entranced, they gathered around the monolith, forgetting the hardships of the day, the perils of the approaching dusk, the hunger in their bellies.

2001: A Space Odyssey
Arthur C. Clarke, 1968

When the apes discover the monolith in *2001: A Space Odyssey*, they're awed by its irresistible power, they're entranced by its novelty. The monolith is perhaps the most memorable image in science fiction, and it's also an appropriate metaphor for the charisma of the Internet and especially the World Wide Web. Like the monolith, the World Wide Web is seductive technology. Surfing the Web, you can choose from millions of sites around the world at the click of a mouse. For a modest amount of money, you can create a Home Page and make it available to millions of people. No doubt about it, the World Wide Web is an exciting marketing opportunity.

But before you rush out and set up your site, pause for a minute to figure out your real reasons for using the Internet as a marketing tool. As I discussed in Chapter 1, you must avoid the trap of marketing technopia. Companies that suffer from this affliction become so entranced by the miraculous nature of digital technology that they lose sight of their most important asset — the customer. When pundits proclaim the vast marketing reach of the Internet, they forget most of the world's population doesn't even own a computer. We're still at least a decade away from the time when everyone will be using the Internet. Until then, you have to do some research to understand your digital market. Otherwise, you may create a digital marketing program that's unsuitable for your customer base.

A news magazine recently placed its electronic version on America Online. If one of the magazine's readers wants to access it, they have to have an AOL account, or they have to get one. I wonder how many of the magazine's readers actually have an account on AOL, or whether the publishers bothered to do a study of the digital capabilities of its readers before going online. My guess is that the success of the magazine's electronic version has been limited. Don't make the same mistake.

The next step in the strategic digital marketing process, therefore, is to conduct some research to understand the technical capabilities and preferences of your customers. Before I talk about how this is done, I will start by looking at some market research on the use of online and digital technology in North America.

THE DIGITAL DEMOGRAPHICS

The Internet: A small elite group: During my research for this book, I took a look at more than 20 reports on the usage of the Internet in North America. The results were not consistent and the discrepancies were likely caused by either their different survey methodologies, or by their vested interest in promoting an inflated picture of Internet usage. By combining the results of all the reports, this is my estimate of what the real numbers are (as of April 1998):

- About 70 million people in Canada and the United States over the age of 16 have access to the Internet. This is a 30-percent increase, up from about 45 million in 1996.
- Seventy percent of Internet users in North America access the Web primarily from home.
- About 45 percent of Internet users access the Web from the office at least some of the time
- Forty percent of the online users are women. (It is expected that women will constitute the majority of online users in Canada and the U.S. within a few years.)
- About 35 percent of Internet users have incomes between $50,000 and $60,000.
- About 75 percent of Internet users have incomes of more than $50,000.
- About 25 percent of Internet users are "newbies," people who went online for the first time in 1997.
- Almost 60 percent of Internet users are between the ages of 35 and 54.
- A large portion of the Internet users who went online in 1997 were from older, less educated, and lower income groups. (This indicates a penetration of the Internet into more mainstream sectors of the Canadian and U.S. economies.)
- About 3.5 million (17 percent) of online users in the United States purchased merchandise or services on the Web in 1997.
- The average online purchase was $100.
- Internet users over 50 years old and women are more likely to buy merchandise and services online.
- Business use of the Internet is expected to grow by more than 500 percent in 1998 and 1999.
- About 50 percent of online business users use e-mail extensively in their day-to-day business activities.

Although accurate statistics on the use of the Internet are difficult to obtain, two relevant trends about the Internet are apparent. The Internet is used actively only by a small percentage of the population, and those users are predominately an elite group comprised of affluent, university-educated people. The size of the Internet will continue to grow, but I'm convinced its rate of growth will begin to plateau. Predictions that there will be a billion users of the Internet by the year 2000 may be overblown. However, new inexpensive Internet-ready telephone/computer terminals (under $500) may bring the Internet into almost every home. As well, the emergence of PotatoNet, spawned by Internet access through television cable, may also increase the Internet's penetration of the total consumer marketplace. However, at the present time, the Internet's market coverage is still only a small share of the total population.

CD-ROM Users: Another elite market: The growth in demand for multimedia products — such as CD-ROM and DVD titles for the entertainment, business, and educational markets — has been fueled in the past few years by the increasing number of computers capable of running multimedia applications through CD-ROM and DVD drives. Research shows that:

- More than 195 million computers worldwide are capable of using multimedia CD-ROMs.
- More than 300,000 DVD drives were sold in 1997, the year they were inrtroduced.
- Sales of DVD drives are expected to reach 6.7 million in 1998 and 24 million in 1999.
- The new media home entertainment industry generates about $8 billion in revenues annually, more than the box office earnings generated by all the motion picture studios combined.
- More than 46,000 CD-ROM titles were available worldwide at the end of 1997. Total DVD titles was 60.

* Source: *InfoTech Report: Optical Publishing Industry Assessment.* For full report, call 1-802-763-2097.

As you can see, the use of CD-ROMs mirrors the demographics of Internet users. It's safe to say that many of these people are users of both CD-ROMs and the Internet. This elite segment of the population are the people who use high-end computers at work, and have the money to buy $3,000 computers for their homes. Until the use of multimedia and online services is delivered via cable modem right to your television set, the consumer market for the Internet and CD-ROM promotions will remain relatively small compared to the total population.

I present these statistics to illustrate the importance of understanding your customers. If your target audience does not use the Internet, a Web site may not be the best tool for your digital marketing program. You might be better off to use a reverse 1-900 number and pay people to listen to your advertising on their telephone, or participate in a cross-promotion with a major credit card company. The thing to remember is: you can market your products and services using digital technology even if none of your customers uses the Internet.

So how do you begin to understand the technical capabilities and preferences of your customers? I suggest you conduct a digital communications audit.

THE DIGITAL COMMUNICATIONS AUDIT

Recently, my company conducted a digital communications audit for an association of 300 nursing home operators. The association wanted to move into the digital age, but they had no idea what technology to use. We conducted a survey of their membership to see what digital tools they use, and what digital information they would like to get from the association in the future. We distributed a survey to each nursing home operator and interviewed 30 of them by telephone or in person. The results of the survey helped the association establish a five-year plan and gave them a much better idea what digital tools they should use to communicate with their members. In the long-term, the cost of the audit will save them thousands of dollars that might have been wasted on trial-and-error digital initiatives. If you wish to conduct a digital communications audit, here are some suggestions:

Quantitative survey: You can prepare a survey and mail or fax it to your target audience. If you're a retailer, you can make the survey available in your store. You can ask many different questions, but make sure that the following ones are included:

Computer Usage
Do you own or have access to a computer?
  At work?
  At home?
  At school?
  Other ___________

If Yes, what kind of computer do you use?
PC with DOS?
PC with Windows 3.1?
PC with Windows 95 or higher?
Macintosh?
Other ___________

If No, are you planning to purchase a computer?

Online Capabilities
Do you have a modem connected to your computer?
What is the speed of the modem?
  (2,400/14.4/28.8/Other)
Do you have an Internet account?
Do you use the World Wide Web?
Does your company have a registered Internet domain name?
Does your company have a World Wide Web site?
Do you use any major online services?
  (CompuServe/America Online/Prodigy)

Do you have an e-mail address?
If No, are you or your company thinking of setting up an e-mail system?

Multimedia Capabilities
How much RAM does your computer have? (4/8/16/32 megs)
Does your PC have a 386, a 486, or 586 (Pentium) processor?
Is your Macintosh a PowerPC?
Do you have a CD-ROM drive on your computer?
Do you have a DVD drive on your computer?
Do you use CD-ROMs for business purposes?
Do you use CD-ROMs for recreational purposes?
Do you have a sound card on your computer?
Can your computer run digital video?

Digital Preferences
Would you like to communicate electronically with us?
Would you use the World Wide Web to get information about us?
Would you like to use a BBS network to connect with us?
Can we put you on our e-mail mailing list?
Would you like to get information from us by fax machine?
Would you like to use your telephone to get information about us?

Information Interests
If we set up an electronic information system, what type of information would you like to receive from us:

Detailed descriptions of our products and services?
Technical specifications and manuals?
Information about our industry, including our competitors?
Other ____________

Do you have information you would like to share with our other customers?

Of course, you would add other questions pertaining directly to your company and customers. You're trying to find out what computer capabilities your customers have, and the information they want. You might find that hardly any of your customers use computers, or that a majority of them have multimedia computers with high-speed modems. It depends on your market.

A calling card survey: If you send out your survey by mail or fax, you should give people an incentive to fill it out. You could give each respondent a financial reward or an opportunity to win a prize. The more people who complete the survey, the more accurate a picture it will give you.

Of course, you could use digital technology to get your survey done. You could mail out a complementary long-distance calling card along with a letter explaining the purpose of your digital audit. The respondent is invited to activate his or her card (for 25 minutes of long distance) by calling a 1-800 number. The respondent answers the questions on the survey with the Touch-Tone keys. They can give verbal answers as well. Once they have completed the survey, they get the free long-distance calls. A calling card survey is very efficient because it will probably yield a higher response rate, and it allows you to collect the data electronically and transfer it directly into your customer database.

Qualitative one-to-one survey: In addition to a written survey, you can interview your customers in person or by telephone. You can go into much greater detail, especially in the area of information preferences. This qualitative survey can be handled as a special project, or it can be coupled with other telemarketing and customer service programs. For example, your salespeople can be trained to ask these questions when they meet with a customer or a prospect. Outbound telemarketing representatives can ask these questions while speaking with customers on routine calls. You can include five or six key questions on order forms or applications. Almost any contact with the customer can be used to gather information for your digital communications audit.

Random sampling: If your target market is narrowly focused, such as a business-to-business market, you may be able to survey almost everyone in your target market. If your market is more widespread, such as the consumer products market, then you will probably need to conduct a random sampling of your market. If you need to conduct such a random sampling, I advise you to work with a qualified research company to conduct your digital communications audit.

The results of the audit: When you have compiled the results of your digital communications audit, you will know which digital tools to use, and which ones to put farther down the list. You will know if an Internet promotional program is appropriate, or whether you should use other digital tools.

THE POPULARITY OF DIGITAL DEVICES

From your digital communications audit, you may learn that very few of your customers would use the World Wide Web to get information from your company. But that doesn't mean you have to abandon digital marketing. There are many other digital devices you can use instead of the World Wide Web. Here's a list of digital marketing tools and their popularity in North America:

Digital tools everyone can use

The Telephone
- Long-Distance Calling Card
- Interactive Voice Response (IVR)
- Audio Mailbox
- 1-800 Line
- Reverse 1-900 Line

Interactive Kiosks
- In-store surveys
- Electronic in-store shopping

Smart Cards
- Loyalty Programs
- Point-of-sale tracking

Digital Coupons

Digital tools many business people use

The Internet
- E-mail
- World Wide Web

Fax Machines
- Fax-on-demand systems
- Fax mailboxes

Cellular Telephones
- Cellular IVR systems
- Direct broadcast (Cellular radio)
- Bulletin Board Services
- Private online networks
- Electronic customer networks

CD-ROM
- Electronic catalogues
- Reference material
- Electronic brochures

Multimedia Presentations and Custom Software
- CD-ROM
- Floppy disk
- Laptop computer
- Screen Savers

Digital tools used by small, but growing, numbers of consumers

The Internet
- World Wide Web
- E-mail

CD-ROM
Multimedia Productions
Promotional Computer Disks
Video Game Players

Digital tools that will have to wait a little longer

Interactive Television
Virtual Reality
Video-Mail
Personal Digital Assistants (PDA)
Inexpensive Internet Terminals

As you can see, the Internet is not the only game in town. You can create an effective digital marketing program using digital telephone technology, smart cards, in-store kiosks, and digital coupons. Or you can combine many of these tools into a wide-reaching digital marketing program. It all depends on the technical capabilities of your customers. I will discuss in detail each of these digital tools in Chapter 8 — Choose Your Digital Tools.

Once you have determined the technical capabilities of your customers, your next step is to begin building your customer database.

CHAPTER 7

START YOUR CUSTOMER DATABASE

The solar system seems to be full of chrono-synclastic infundibulum. There is one big one we are sure of that likes to stay between Earth and Mars. Chrono (kroh-no) means time. Synclastic (sin-class-tick) means curved toward the same side in all directions, like the skin of an orange. Infundibulum (in-fun-dib-u-lum) is what the ancient Romans like Julius Caesar and Nero called a funnel. If you don't know what a funnel is, get Mommy to show you one.

The Sirens of Titan
Kurt Vonnegut, 1959

A customer database is like Kurt Vonnegut's chrono-synclastic infundibulum. It takes time to build, it curves in all directions, it's like a funnel, and it spans the known universe — your marketing universe, that is. A customer database is the fundamental tool of digital marketing. By keeping an accurate profile of your customers, a database will help you develop better relationships with them on a one-to-one basis. You'll be able to better serve their needs and communicate more effectively with them. Before I discuss how to set up your customer database, I'll explain briefly the basic features of database technology.

HOW DATABASES WORK

A digital filing cabinet: Think of a database as an electronic filing cabinet. In a filing cabinet, you store information about your customers on pieces of paper such as order forms, invoices, and account statements. The forms contain the customer's name, address, and telephone number, along with all sorts of other information. To help you find them, you store the forms in alphabetical order by name, or in chronological order by date of purchase of your products and services. You also group them together into file folders. If you want to find some information about the customer, you go to the filing cabinet and pull out the form. If your filing system has been well designed, you can find the information you want quickly.

The problem with a print-based filing system is its lack of versatility. If you want to know how many of your customers live in New York City, you have to pull out all your files to look at each address. If you want to know how many customers spend more than $1,000 a year on your products and services, you have to do the same thing. This is a very time-consuming and expensive process. If you want to send a letter to your customers, you have to pull out the forms, type up the letters, and type up the address labels. This is also a very arduous task. In addition, if you want to get information from the filing cabinet, you need to be where it's located. For example, if your head office is in Montreal and you're working in Los Angeles, you don't have ready access to your customer records. Obviously, a print-based filing system has its limitations, but it was the only method possible before the advent of computers and database software.

Fields to be harvested: Database software allows you to store information about your customers on computer in an electronic form. A simple customer database might contain the following information about each of your customers:

First name
Last name
Title
Company
Address
City
Telephone #
Fax #

Each of these lines is contained in a separate compartment known as a "field." You put the person's name in the Name field. You put the person's telephone number in the Telephone field. If you want to keep track of the person's gender, you add a Sex field.

This type of database is useful for many things. You can print out a list of your customers in alphabetical order, by name, or by company. You can use the database to look in the City field and find only those customers who live in Chicago. You can be more selective and ask the database to give you a list of your customers in Chicago with the first name Fred. This simple customer database can also be used to print letters and mailing labels.

The key feature of database software is the fact that each piece of information is stored in a separate field. If you put your customer information into a word processing document, you can print out the list and perhaps print out labels, but you can't rearrange the information in any other way. By breaking down the information into fields, you can rearrange and manipulate it in any way you want. As well, you can add additional fields to give you even more detailed information about your customers.

My company has developed hundreds of customer databases for companies large and small. For one client, we created an extensive customer database of people involved in the Canadian motion picture and television industry. The database contains the names and addresses of more than 5,000 film and television professionals in the country including directors of photography, and key contacts at film processing labs, editing facilities, and film distribution companies.

Each person on the list has a special code placed in a field called "Line-of-Business." Directors of photography are given the code DP, the lab technicians are given the code LT, and the editors are given the code ED. If we want to send a special promotional package to the lab technicians, we ask the database to display a list of only those people who have the code LT in the Line-of-Business field. The database also contains information received from a reply card distributed in a printed newsletter. On the reply card, customers indicate the type of information they want to receive, and any comments they wish to make. All of the survey results are stored in the database.

As you develop your customer database, you can add additional fields over time. You may wish to begin with a simple mailing list, and then start adding other information you deem appropriate. If you run a small business, you may start out with only 100 names and addresses, but soon find you have more than 5,000 records with dozens of different fields. If you're in a large corporation, your database may contain millions of customers. The key point is that you can start off with a relatively modest customer database and move toward greater sophistication. You don't need to be a large corporation to use a customer database.

Relational databases: The type of database I described in the previous section is called a flatline database. This means each database you have is an island unto itself. For example, you might have two databases: a customer mailing list, and another one that keeps track of purchases. Because both involve customers, you have duplicate information about the same people in each database. If a customer moves, you have to go into both databases to change the person's address and telephone number. In other words, there is no relationship between the two databases. Using a number of different flatline databases might be adequate when you're running a relatively modest operation, but it's a nightmare if your company has thousands of customers, and numerous departments, spread across the country. The process of keeping each database up to date and in sync with the others becomes too difficult. At some point, you need to link them into a *relational* database format.

A relational database allows you to link all the databases run by your company. For example, you might have a database for each of these areas:

- a customer mailing list;
- a list of sales prospects;
- invoicing and purchasing records;
- responses to customer surveys; and
- a list of customers who redeem coupons.

Using relational database software, you can link up the information from each of these separate databases. From within your customer mailing list, you can see what information is contained about a customer in the invoicing record, and what her responses were to a survey. You don't need to jump back and forth between separate databases. If you are creating an invoice, you simply type in the person's name and her address appears on the screen. The computer has looked for that person in the customer mailing list. For this reason, you only need to keep one record of the person's address and telephone number. If a customer moves, you don't have to go into five different databases to change her address. It's much more efficient, and provides you with a much greater wealth of ready-to-use information about the customer.

If you're planning to expand your business, I recommend you purchase *relational* rather than *flatline* database software. It will allow you to continuously integrate new information and give you greater flexibility. The cost of relational database software is falling, so the price should not be a major barrier. You don't need to be a big company to use a relational database.

WHY YOU NEED A CUSTOMER DATABASE

If you want to market effectively in the digital age, you need to give customers what they want: custom-tailored products, one-to-one service, acknowledgment of their importance, and what I call "The Old Neighborhood Store Feeling." To do this, you need to have a customer database.

Custom-tailored products: The more information you have about your customers, the more creative you can be in developing products and services that are custom tailored to their individual needs. If your database tells you that 20 percent of your customers are retired and enjoy traveling south in the winter, you can offer them customized travel packages to Florida and the Caribbean. If you know that 65 percent of your customers do their own home repairs, you can create a Do-It-Yourself promotion aimed only at them. If you know that 5,523 of your customers enjoy watching science fiction movies, you can create a specialized Sci-Fi Lovers Club at your video store. Using surveys to build your database, you can gather more and more information about your customers. Do they like low-fat foods? Do they exercise three or more times a week? Do they read to their children? Do they know how to operate a computer? Do they spend more than $100 a month on long-distance phone calls? With statistics like these, you can create special products. In fact, a customer database enables you to create a different product or service for each person.

Personalized service: A database allows you to keep track of your customers' special needs and desires. Let's say you operate a hotel. When customers visit your hotel, they expect personalized service. They want you to wake them up at 6:15 a.m., bring them *The New York Times*, and arrange a workout with a personal trainer. They want a fax machine in their room and extra towels in the bathroom. If you have this information in a database, you already know what special services the guests want before they arrive. If you don't have a database, they have to tell you every time they come to your hotel. After a while, guests may tire of telling you what they want and go to a hotel that remembers their special requests. This is just one example of how a database can help you deliver personalized service.

Databases can help a publisher of information such as a magazine or a television network deliver custom information to each of its subscribers. The best example of this process, called PUSH, is *The Pointcast Network* (www.pointcast.com). As a free subscriber, you choose the type of news you wish to receive. You indicate what company stock prices you want to monitor and what international news you want to follow. At regular intervals, the service sends you (pushes) the personalized information you requested to your computer — along with advertising messages. It's like having your own personal newspaper delivered right to your computer. What makes this system work, of course, is a database that keeps track of all subscribers and what they want to see on their desktop.

If you're a small business, a customer database will help you provide personalized service. Even if you only have 100 regular customers, and 200 occasional customers, you still have a large number of people to keep track of. For example, a florist might keep track of the dates that are important in each of his customer's lives. Customers are called a week before birthdays, anniversaries, or holidays with floral gift suggestions. Customers will be duly impressed and, if they're like me, thankful for the reminder. Although you could keep track of these dates on paper, the database allows you to track hundreds of dates and hundreds of people, faster and more easily.

Acknowledgment of their importance: Have you ever heard one of your customers say: "I've been a customer here for ten years and you treat me like this? I can't believe you're treating me like this." If so, you need a customer database. It will help you identify your longtime customers and acknowledge how important they are to you. You can create a loyalty program and reward them with discounts, prizes or air miles, or any of a multitude of premiums and incentives. You can keep track of their children's names and their favorite color. You can electronically remember they have a sinus condition and ask them about it when they visit your store during allergy season.

Keeping track of your best customers in a database is especially important when your operation is large and potentially impersonal.

If you hire new salespeople, they won't know that Mrs. Oldmoney has been shopping at your store since electricity was invented. But if they can look her up in a database, the green recruits will be alerted to Mrs. Oldmoney's special status. And if you link your customer database up between stores, Mrs. Oldmoney can be treated like an empress at all the shops in your chain.

The old neighborhood store feeling: Remember when you used to shop at Mr. Farley's Grocery Store around the corner from your house? Mr. Farley knew your mom was expecting another baby, and your dad just got a new job. When you went to pick up the milk, he gave you some ice cream to take home because he knew your sister was sick. Now think about these days. You shop at the Warehouse Discount Store along with thousands of other people. You don't know anybody at the store, and they don't know you. You save a few dollars, but you feel empty and a little depressed when you drive away. Somehow, you'd like to get the advantages of a large retail store — lower prices and wide selection — and the advantages of a neighborhood store — personal attention and an understanding of your special needs.

The answer is a customer database. When you go into a department store, they ask you for your membership card. The card is linked to the database and tells the salesperson who you are and what your preferences are. The salesperson suggests some special items recently made available, or shows them to you. You feel like someone is acknowledging that you are a unique individual who is important to the store. Although we will probably never return to the days of Mr. Farley's Grocery Store, customer databases can help make the large department stores warmer, more personable places to shop.

BENEFITS YOU WILL REALIZE FROM A CUSTOMER DATABASE

Higher level of repeat business: Your best source of new business is your existing customer base. It costs many times more to find new customers than it does to keep them. If you use a customer database properly, you can communicate with your customers more often, and serve their needs better. For example, you could create an e-mail newsletter that goes out to your customers on a weekly basis. You would simply draw the e-mail addresses from your customer database and send the message out using one of the popular e-mail software programs. Because e-mail is so inexpensive to transmit, you can communicate with your customers more often for less money. The increased level of contact with the customer is sure to increase their awareness of your business, and result in a higher level of repeat business.

Lower promotional and sales costs: If you can get most of your revenue from existing customers, you can lower your cost of prospecting. You can also target only people who are interested. For example, if you are selling sophisticated Night Vision Binoculars to bird watchers, you could advertise in *Bird Watching World* magazine or you could send out a newsletter by fax or e-mail. The cost of the magazine advertising would be much higher in relative terms than the e-mail or fax. As well, many of the magazine's readers either have night vision binoculars, or they don't watch birds at night. This is called wasted circulation. Using your customer database, you can send out promotional literature to those people who said, in your last survey, that they would like to do night bird watching, but don't have the right equipment. Your response to this kind of target promotion will be much better, per dollar spent, than it could ever have been in a magazine ad. (An ad in *Bird Watching World* might be a good idea to reach new bird watchers who have never heard of your company. The ad could be used to entice readers to call in and fill out your interactive telephone survey, or log into your Web site to fill in your online questionnaire. This will get them into your database, and you will discover if they want to join the growing ranks of nocturnal owl chasers.)

Lower market research costs: A customer database will help you lower market research costs. As I said in Chapter 2, market research is an ongoing, interactive process in the digital marketing environment. You are constantly gathering information from your customers and prospects to be used in developing new products and services. Salespeople ask clients questions when they make sales calls. The answers are entered into laptop computers and uploaded each night to the central customer database. Inbound telemarketers ask questions of people who call to get technical information about a new product. Your customer service representatives ask questions when they field complaints. Every contact with the customer is used to add to your database and, as you gather more and more data, it becomes less necessary to conduct formal quantitative and qualitative research studies. That's because you already know your customers want a faster product that's easier to repair. You already know your clients on the West Coast are more price conscious than your clients on the East Coast. You already know your customers want more chocolate chips in their cookies. In fact, maintaining a customer database not only lowers the cost of traditional market research — it can make it irrelevant and unnecessary.

Access to just-in-time information: If you constantly gather content for your customer database, you'll be better equipped to get the information you need when you need it. Let's say, for example, you get a call from a wholesaler who has 100 size-12 basketball shoes for sale. He will give you 75 percent off, but you have to place the order today. You look into your customer database and discover you have more than 3,400 customers with size-12 feet who play basketball and haven't bought new shoes in over a year. You call the wholesaler right back and place the order. To generate sales you send out an e-mail message to your customers with big feet. You tell them a special purchase has been made with them in mind. Within hours you receive 75 responses and sell out the order in a matter of days.

HOW TO SET UP YOUR CUSTOMER DATABASE

Your database team: If you're planning a large-scale database project, you'll need to form a team of people to handle its implementation and ongoing maintenance. You need people to manage:

- the hardware, software, and input/output devices;
- the content and structure of the database; and
- the development of promotional programs.

To make it work, your customer database project needs to have the support of your entire organization. Bring in people from other departments such as customer service, market research, sales, and personnel. Keep in mind, however, that this is not strictly a technical endeavor. Don't just hand the project over to your computer people. Develop your marketing strategy first, and then get the computer people to create a system to help you implement the strategy.

If you run a small business, you'll have to handle these activities yourself or get help from a consultant. Either way, the development of a customer database is a relatively simple process for a small business.

Hardware and software: In a large corporation, the hardware and software required to establish a customer database system can cost millions of dollars and take many months, even years, to implement. To work properly, the database must be an integrated part of your Information Technology (IT) system. In many cases, your IT system may not be advanced enough to deliver the results you require. If your company is contemplating a new IT system, make sure you put forward your plan for the customer database to the IT selection committee. You want to make sure that the new system will have these features:

- The database is relational (all customer databases can be linked together).
- Everyone in the company can access the customer database from their PC.

- You can continuously change and update content.
- You can easily generate reports at any time.
- The storage capacity of the server is large enough to accommodate a large and growing amount of information.
- The database can be linked to your input and output devices such as your Web site, your BBS, your 1-800 telephone IVR system, your point-of-sale system, and your e-mail and fax broadcast system.
- Additional input and output devices can be incorporated as needed in the future.

If you're running a small business, you'll require the following:

- relational database software;
- a computer with a 486 or faster processor;
- 8 megs of RAM;
- a large-capacity hard drive with at least 500 megs of storage;
- a backup hard drive and/or removable drive (back up your database on a daily or weekly basis and consider using a removable drive so you can guard against fire or theft by storing the copies in alternate locations);
- A laser or dot matrix printer for preparing mailing labels.

Field structure: Once you have your hardware and software installed, you begin your database by setting up the fields you want to use. As I discussed, the standard fields include first name, last name, address, telephone number, fax, and so on (e-mail addresses are fast becoming a standard database field). You can add any additional fields you want such as gender, line of business, income level, number of children, color of hair, or type of car. Don't hold back. Add as many fields as possible. Although you can always add new fields later, it's better if you put in most of the fields you need upfront.

The old shoe box: If you've never used a database before, you probably have all your customer information in print form — business cards, invoices, faxes. (I had one client at a large manufacturing company who had information about his customers stuffed in an old shoe box.) Your task is to enter all this information into your new database. This job is a very boring and time-consuming process, so you may want to hire someone to do it.

If you already have a customer database, but want to upgrade your software to a relational format, you can probably convert and import the data into the new database. This is a relatively simple process, but it does require some expertise. You might consider hiring a consultant to handle this conversion.

Segmentation and coding: When you're setting up your fields, divide your market into a number of different groups or segments. For example, as an insurance agent, you might divide your market into two groups: Home Owners and Renters. To keep track of the two segments in your database, you create a field called Owner/Renter. In this field you enter HO (Home Owner) or R (Renter) for each person. When you want to send out some information about tenant insurance, you ask the database to give you a list of renters. You can create a subsegment for the renters and create a field called Apartment/House, and enter an A for apartment or H for house. This allows you to target the apartment renters with special promotions and unique products. This is a very simple example, but it illustrates the principle. You can create as many segments and subsegments as you want.

Getting it right: If you're going to keep a customer database, you must dot your "i's" and cross your "t's." There is nothing more aggravating than receiving a personalized letter with your name misspelled. Recently I received a promotion from a business newspaper that used a database to print out a headline with my name on it. However, the headline read "Bill B. Ishop Wins Grand Prize." It was ridiculous, and a perfect example of how database marketing can go terribly wrong if the information is inaccurate.

Adding prospect names: Once you have all your existing customers in the database, you may wish to add prospect names to the list. List brokers can provide you with data on individuals and companies in your target market. You can get a list of people in your city who have incomes in excess of $300,000 a year, or a list of businesses with more than 50 employees and revenues of more than $20 million a year. These lists can be purchased in an electronic format and imported into your database. If you don't want to pay a list broker, you can add names to the list by going through the Yellow Pages, industry association directories, and trade magazines. You might also link up with businesses who target the same market, and share your databases with each other. (We will look at the ethical implications of database sharing in Section Four.)

ATTRACT MORE CUSTOMERS AND HAVE BETTER RELATIONSHIPS

Publish a newsletter: If you want to use your database to communicate more effectively with your customers, I suggest you start publishing a newsletter which can be printed and mailed, broadcast by fax, or distributed by e-mail. When developing your database, ask customers if they would like to receive your newsletter, and how they would like to receive it: mail, fax, or e-mail? If you ask permission first, your customers won't consider your newsletter to be junk mail. In the newsletter, include a reply card along with an incentive to fill out the questions.

Remember your prime objective: In Chapter 8, I will look at digital tools, such as customer loyalty cards, a World Wide Web site, a BBS, and an interactive voice-response system which you can use to feed information into your customer database. In Chapter 9, I will discuss promotional ideas you can use to draw people into your digital domain. But remember, the point isn't simply to gather names of people and the type of orange juice they drink. The ultimate objective is to attract more customers, and to have better relationships with them. If you have a customer database in place, you're on your way to achieving this goal.

CHAPTER 8

CHOOSE YOUR DIGITAL TOOLS

The Three Laws of Robotics: 1. A robot may not injure a human being, or, through inaction, allow a human being to come to harm. 2. A robot must obey the orders given to it by human beings except where such orders would conflict with the First Law. 3. A robot must protect its own existence as long as such protection does not conflict with the First or Second Law.

I, Robot
Isaac Asimov, 1950

Isaac Asimov developed the Three Laws of Robotics and wrote a series of books exploring the relationship between humans and robots. As a digital marketer, you must also understand your relationship with robot-like tools such as computers, databases, smart cards, and the Internet. So before I explain the digital tools you can use for marketing, I wish to propose these Three Laws of Digital Marketing:

1. A digital marketing tool may not ruin a company, or, through inaction, allow a company to be ruined.

2. A digital marketing tool must be used to achieve business objectives, except where such objectives would conflict with the First Law.
3. A digital marketing tool must be chosen as part of a marketing strategy, as long as the strategy does not conflict with the First or Second Law.

If you obey these laws, you will have a much better chance of succeeding at digital marketing. Don't choose a digital tool because it's the latest fad, and don't take the first one that comes along. Look at all the digital marketing tools and choose the ones most appropriate for your company and your customers.

THE TELEPHONE: EVERYONE USES ONE

The telephone is the most powerful digital marketing tool because just about everyone uses one. It's safe to say that 99.9 percent of the people in your target market use a telephone. If you use a digital telephone tool to promote your company, you can be sure that everyone will be able to access it.

The telephone became a digital tool in the 1970s with the advent of digital switching; that's when you traded in your rotary dial telephone for one with Touch-Tone keys. That's when the telephone became a digital device allowing you to store and retrieve voice mail messages, fulfill banking transactions, order courier pickups, or join dating chat lines. Your telephone company has introduced dozens of new options including: toll-free 1-800 lines, pay-per-use 1-900 services, call answer, call display, call waiting, and many others. Let's take a look at each of the digital telephone services and examine how they can be used for marketing.

Voice mail: If you're in business, it's likely your company has voice mail. In most cases, voice mail is used solely to store messages, but it can be used for so much more. You can use voice mail to:

- **Provide detailed information about your company and its services.** In addition to the regular options, your voice mail system may offer callers a submenu. For example, by selecting "6" on their Touch-Tone keypad, your customers can listen to a brief description of each of your products and services. Although this sounds like a really simple idea, very few companies use their voice mail for this purpose.
- **Provide late-breaking news.** You could post a daily message to your voice mail system telling callers about such things as a one-day surprise sale, a new product launch, the opening of a new location, or any other late-breaking story.
- **Process orders.** For years, my company has used the voice mail system at Federal Express to order couriers. We call FedEx and enter our account number. We answer a number of different questions using the Touch-Tone keys, and the computer voice confirms our order. We never speak to a person, although we have that option at any time. We prefer this system because it is faster and more accurate than dealing with a live order taker. Like FedEx, your company can use its voice mail system to automate order taking. Some people will prefer using it because they enjoy buying anonymously. They don't like speaking with salespeople who might pressure them into buying something they don't want.
- **Gather content for your customer database.** By linking your voice mail system directly to your customer database, you can gather additional information from existing clients and new information about prospective clients. For example, the caller can select "7" to enter a contest to win a new motor home. To be eligible, they must answer five questions using the Touch-Tone keys, and provide their name, address, telephone number, and e-mail address. All this information can be sent immediately to your customer database.
- **Provide answers to technical questions.** If you receive a large number of customer enquiries about your products or services, you can use your voice mail to provide answers to the most commonly asked questions. This will speed up the

process for your customers, and allow you to service customers with less staff.

- **Set up personal voice mail boxes for your customers.** You can create voice mail boxes on your system for your best customers. The customers tell you what kind of information they want, and you gather it and place it in their mailboxes. They can retrieve the messages whenever they want, wherever they want — from their home, their office, or cellular telephone. It would be like having a private, customized radio news service. For example, a financial services company can offer customized investment and economic information. Each customer can indicate which news best fits their personal criteria and are free to call the service at any time, day or night. This service can be used as a promotional tool and offered for free or as part of a revenue generating service package.
- **Provide instant testimonials.** Why not get your most satisfied customers to say something nice about your company and place the message on your voice mail system? "To hear what our customers have to say about us, press '9'."
- **Create an interactive news show.** Instead of printing your newsletter, why not produce a news show on your voice mail system? You can have interviews with your customers, and your employees, along with guest appearances by celebrities or well-known industry experts. The caller can be directed through the show using voice mail menu options. This idea will work best if you provide some incentive for calling, either a financial reward or the pleasure of listening to high-quality, entertaining, and valuable content.
- **Provide customized, interactive information.** You can use your voice mail system to give answers to specific questions. For example, if you're an auto dealer, you could give callers the location of your nearest dealership. The caller would simply enter her area code to receive the answer. A children's book publisher can set up a system that asks the caller the age of her children. The caller receives back a customized menu describing books for children in those age groups. A pharmacy can set up a system

asking callers to choose from a variety of over-the-counter medications and then provide information on how to use them.

Voice mail broadcast: When creating your customer database, ask people if they would like to receive information by telephone. Would they like to receive a voice mail broadcast about their stock portfolio on a daily or weekly basis? Would they like to receive a message about last-minute vacation deals? Would they like to hear about sales at a store they patronize? You can either make the calls one at a time, or you can send out the messages using automated voice mail broadcast technology. The system will store the messages you want to send out, and then call up the people on the list and broadcast the message. If people request to receive information in this way, they won't think of it as an irritating intrusion.

As you can see, there are many ways you can use your voice mail for marketing purposes. And, if you already have a voice mail system, you won't need to pay for any new equipment.

A 1-900 number: 1-800 toll-free has become a popular way to encourage people to call your company because you pick up the long-distance charges. With 1-900, it is the opposite. The caller picks up the tab for the call, and usually pays more than the long-distance fare. These services have become a popular way to peddle telephone dating services, sex chats, horoscopes, and soap opera highlights. For digital marketing, you could use a 1-900 number to:

- **Run a contest:** Build your database by running a contest for a Trip Around The World. To enter, the caller must dial your 1-900 number. They listen to a Hollywood movie star or a sports celebrity describe the trip, and then enter the contest by answering questions by voice and Touch-Tone dial. The money raised by the 1-900 can be used to defray the cost of the promotion, or can be given to a charity.
- **Operate a consumer advice service:** Computer consulting companies, for example, can set up an advice service billed through a 1-900 number. If you have a question about your

computer, you call the number and speak to a consultant. Instead of receiving an invoice in the mail, the per-minute charges are put on your phone bill. The service provider, on the other hand, receives a cheque from the telephone company.

- **Broadcast a business-to-business news show:** You can set up an information service that provide news and information for your specific industry. If you're an auto parts manufacturer, you can create a 1-900 news show providing daily information about the automotive industry. The callers will pay for the 1-900 service if the information is timely, accurate, and can't be found anywhere else. This type of service can be used for almost any trade sector. Of course, you can also provide this service on a 1-800 number, but making it a pay-per-use service will raise its credibility.

If you plan to use a 1-900 number to set up a new service or to run a promotion, make sure you put a lot of effort into developing quality content. Make it entertaining or extremely useful. You want your callers to keep calling back time and time again.

Reverse 1-900: With a reverse 1-900 number, you pay the caller to call you. Instead of receiving a charge on his telephone bill, the caller receives a credit for calling you. Sound absurd? Well, suppose you want people to hear about your new product. You can buy radio and television ads or put up a billboard. Either way, you are paying people to read your ad, so why not do it over the telephone? And more importantly, you can use the opportunity to do market research and gather information for your customer database. You would actually be paying people to call your number and answer a series of questions; you can't do that with a radio ad.

Let's look at a possible scenario. You are thinking about launching a new kind of laundry detergent. You distribute a flyer in a local newspaper, or through the billing envelope for the telephone company. The flyer invites people to call a reverse 1-900 number and receive a credit on their phone bill. When they make the call, they're asked to answer a series of questions. The more questions they answer, the more credit they receive off their bill, so they don't mind answering ten or 20 questions; the more the merrier. You can also throw in some promotional spots about your other products and offer coupons and other rebates.

Pay phone services: This idea takes the reverse 1-900 concept and blows it wide open. You can set up a service that pays people to listen to advertising messages on the telephone. To subscribe, the person first fills out a detailed survey. (This can be done by interactive telephone as well.) Each time he picks up the telephone, a voice comes on and asks him if he would like to earn some money before making the call. If yes, the caller listens to a series of advertising messages, and responds to various prompts to make sure he's actually listening. The advertisements are selected based on the replies he made to the sign-up survey. He can also elect to receive coupons and product brochures at the end of each message. At the end of each month, the subscriber receives his telephone bill. If he has been listening to enough messages, the balance could be zero or even positive. He also receives a package of the coupons and product literature he requested.

In addition, the service can intercept any calls he makes to competitors. For example, if he tries to call Speedy Muffler, a voice comes on the line and tells him that Midas Muffler has a special promotion on, and will pay him 25 percent off if he reroutes his call to Midas. While this may sound high-handed, the subscriber would be asked upfront if he would like to participate in this type of cross-calling. If not, he would not have his calls intercepted.

You could set up your own Pay Phone system, or join up with a service bureau. A large department store or retail chain, for example, could set up its own system. Its customers would be invited to join the Pay Phone Club, and listen to daily messages about the store's products and services. To defray the costs, the department store can charge its suppliers to participate.

This type of Pay Phone system has been introduced in several US cities, but has yet to be offered in Canada.

Prepaid long-distance calling cards: These cards are catching on in North America after many years of popularity in Europe and Asia. You buy the cards in a store, and they entitle you to a certain amount of long-distance calling time. Once the time is used up, you throw the card away or keep it as a collector's item. (Note: Calling card collecting has become a huge business. There are dozens of magazines and trade shows dedicated to this hobby.)

You can create a $25 prepaid calling card for your business, the Pet Travel company. You hand out the card, with your pet logo on it, to your best customers and prospects. When the user dials up the 1-800 number, they are asked to enter the PIN number on the card. A voice comes on and says, "Is your dog or cat bored? Do they dream of far-off places? Of course they do. They're sick and tired of being stuck in the house all day while you're at the office. So before we activate your card, we invite you to listen to a few words about our pet travel services." Once the message is over, and they've heard about your Canine-only Mediterranean Cruise Special, the caller may place her call to anywhere in North America. She's entitled to $25 worth of calling, and can use the card until all of the time has been spent. The caller is also invited to connect directly with a Pet Travel reservation representative at any time during the call, or to join the Pet Travel Club.

You can use a Calling Card promotion for almost any audience, but it is primarily applicable for well-defined markets with products and services of high value. It is ideal for a business-to-business market in which people travel and make long-distance calls. It is also useful for hard-to-reach prospects such as company presidents. Keep in mind you don't need to use an actual card for this type of promotion: you can send out a letter with the PIN number on it. However, the card has more impact because it is portable and durable, and has a perceived intrinsic value.

Cellular telephones: The use of cellular telephones has skyrocketed since they were introduced in the mid-1980s. There are two major types: the handheld portable model and the hands-free in-car model. You can create special digital promotions for both of these.

- **Hands-free in-car cellular telephones**: When people are in the car and driving to work, they don't have much to do but listen to the radio, so why not turn their cellular telephone into a radio plugged directly into you? As a business consulting company, you can advertise on roadside billboards that you have a special cellular service for business people. They can call *88 on their cellular telephone and listen to a morning news show. The caller doesn't receive a bill for listening because you negotiated a bulk rate with the cellular provider. Callers might even receive a credit on their cellular bill. In addition, you can sell ad spots on your show to other companies in order to pay for the show, and for your bill to the cellular provider.
- **Portable cellular telephones**: Everywhere you look people are walking around with a portable phone to their ear, so why not get them to listen to you instead? You can place advertising on storefronts, billboards, real estate signs, and any other media, and invite people to call *55 to get more information about your product and service. Once again, they would not have to pay for the call, and may receive a credit on their cellular bill. Note: If you are targeting the portable cellular user, keep the messages brief. With the in-car model, you can make the message as long as you want because the listener usually has more time.

As you can see, telephone technology has many digital marketing applications. The key advantage of telephones over other digital tools is everyone uses them. Unlike more advanced digital tools, by using the phone system you don't have to worry if your audience has the equipment to access your information.

DIGITAL CARDS AND COUPONS

A growing area of digital marketing is the use of loyalty programs to identify customers and track their buying habits. Many chain retailers have been running loyalty programs for many years. As a member, you receive points for every purchase and can redeem them at any time for merchandise. By scanning in the loyalty card during each purchase, the retailer gathers detailed information about its customers. It knows what they buy, how often they buy, and how they pay. The growing number of points also helps to keep customers coming back rather than shopping at a competitor's store. You may not have the resources of a national retail chain, but you can still use digital technology to identify and track your customers.

Loyalty club cards: Even if you only operate a single store, you can still create a Best Customer's Club. As a restaurant owner, for example, you can give the card to your best customers and tell them to present it every time they come to your restaurant. The card entitles them to special discounts on meals, air miles, credit at other retail outlets, and so on.

For each member of the club, you set up an account on your customer database. The type of card you use will depend on how much money you want to spend, and the number of accounts you need to administer. These cards include:

- **Magnetic stripe**: These cards have a magnetic stripe on the back, similar to most credit and debit cards. You swipe the card through a device that reads the information on the magnetic stripe which contains information about who owns the card. This data is fed into a computer which calls up the person's account. If the reader is connected to your cash register, both the person's name and her purchases are recorded in the database.
- **Bar codes**: These cards use the universal bar code format to identify the owner of the card. You use your bar code

scanner to read the card. Like the magnetic stripe card, bar code cards can transfer data to the customer database; they can also keep track of purchases.

- **Manual entry**: If you don't want to spend the money on bar code scanners or card stripe readers, you can enter manually the customer card number into your database during each purchase. You can enter manually the amount of the purchase into the computer as well. This might be the best process at first, especially if you have a small volume of customers to deal with.
- **Smart cards**: Although smart cards are in their infancy, they are worth noting here. A smart card is aptly named because it's much smarter than a regular credit card or debit card. A regular card only holds enough information to identify the user and hold a confidential password. A smart card can gather and store a large amount of information; it is like a miniature computer. For example, a smart card can store medical information. Every time a person visits the doctor or buys drugs at a pharmacy, the card updates itself to include the new data. In the event of an accident, the card will tell the attending physicians the person's medical profile. Smart cards can also store digital cash. In the future, when you go to the bank machine, you will "withdraw money" and put it on your smart card. When you make a purchase, the electronic funds will be withdrawn directly from the card.

You can use a smart card as part of your digital marketing program. When the customer buys something at your store, they present their smart card and get points or dollar amounts added onto the card. At any time, they can present the card and buy products with it. (In a few years, they will be able to use the card at home to purchase products online from you, using card readers attached to their telephones, computers, and televisions.) I believe that the smart card is a better tool for a points program than a regular card. Unlike points that accumulate on some far-off computer, smart points accumulate right in your pocket.

They can become a currency in their own right, much the same way Canadian Tire money has practically become a second Canadian currency.

Digital coupons: If you want to keep track of people who redeem your coupons, why not send them digital coupons with a magnetic stripe or bar code on them? You register each coupon on your database before you mail them out to your customers. When your customers redeem and return them, you run the coupons through a high-speed reader — linked to your database — to find out which of your customers redeemed the coupons. You can analyze the results to determine the best strategy for your next coupon promotion. For example, the results might reveal that only men redeem the coupons, or only people who earn less than $30,000 a year. When you run another coupon program, you can simply send the coupons to people who actually use them. The important point is that you can turn your coupons into a digital tool by adding a bar code or magnetic stripe to them, and linking each coupon to a specific customer.

Digital cheques: Why not send out digital cheques rather than coupons? Unlike coupons, cheques are quickly processed, run through the banking system, and have a higher perceived value in the mind of the customer. The cheques are made out to a particular retailer or a group of retailers and can be redeemed for a certain dollar amount off your products. The customers fill out the cheques, and answer the survey questions on the back. When they make the purchase, the retailer deposits the digital cheques along with his other receipts. After receiving the cheques through the banking system, you run them through a scanner which transmits the names and survey answers into your customer database.

A loyalty program or club is an excellent way to increase repeat business and to build a more detailed customer database. If you already have some kind of loyalty program, make sure it's connected to your customer database.

ONLINE TOOLS: NOT JUST THE WEB

The advent of the World Wide Web has created tremendous interest in using online technology for marketing. The Web gives marketers the ability to post a wealth of information on the Internet at a relatively low cost. If you have a basic knowledge of computer technology, you can create a home page and place it on the World Wide Web. And, it is promised, a global market will come knocking on your door.

The World Wide Web is a very powerful digital marketing tool, but it has to be used in the right way. Unfortunately, many companies are using the Web ineffectively. They take the copy and pictures from their brochures and put them on the Web, and then wait for the world to come to them. Then nothing happens. Well, excuse me, but what do they expect? Do they really think people will be thrilled to read their brochure just because it is on the Internet? Do they think people have nothing better to do than surf the Internet all day long just to find out they have five manufacturing plants, 30 stores, and 650 employees?

Some people also fail to realize that currently the Internet is used by less than 20 percent of the population. So unless their customers are part of the Internet community, a Web site isn't going to be effective.

The other mistake people make is they think the World Wide Web *is* the Internet, or even more erroneously, the Web is the Information Superhighway. Well, I know the Information Superhighway, and so far, the Web is no Superhighway. There are many other online marketing tools besides the World Wide Web including e-mail, BBS systems, private networks, list servers, and newsgroups. Depending on your situation, any of these online tools may be the most appropriate for you. Let's take a look at each of them.

The Internet: As I explained in Chapter 4, the Internet is a global computer network and about 20 million people currently use the system for both business and recreation. Commercial promotion was taboo on the Internet only a few years ago when it was used almost exclusively by universities and government agencies. With the advent of the World Wide Web, the Internet grudgingly embraced commercial activity. As such, the Internet now offers many opportunities for the astute marketer.

A. Mighty e-mail: In the 1980s, everyone added fax numbers to their business cards, and in the 1990s they are adding e-mail addresses. Almost everyone, especially business people, will have an e-mail address by the end of the century. By its very nature, e-mail is the most powerful online marketing tool.

Unlike a Web site, which is a passive medium, e-mail is an intrusive medium. Instead of waiting for someone to access your site, you can send them an e-mail message. You can set up an e-mail list and send all your customers an e-mail about next week's sale. You can include electronic coupons and daily specials that can be ordered simply by sending back a reply e-mail message. In fact, you can create a list with thousands of e-mail addresses, and send out an e-mail to all of them in a matter of seconds, at virtually no cost. Imagine if all 50,000 of your customers are on an e-mail list. You wouldn't have to mail out a newsletter or a flyer. You wouldn't have to advertise in a newspaper. You could simply send out e-mail on a regular basis. Your marketing costs would plummet. Because a database makes these e-mail strategies possible, I can't put enough emphasis on the importance of creating a customer database. If your database contains all your customers' e-mail addresses, you can run a marketing program without spending on advertising, postage, long distance, or printing. So, if you haven't started adding e-mail addresses to your customer database, get started now.

B. Mail list servers: If you want to keep your customers informed about your services, and help them communicate with each other, consider setting up a mail list server. Using e-mail, people can subscribe to your list server and receive regular messages from the people who belong to the list.

Let's say you run a company called The Great Fishing Supplies Company. You might want to set up the Fishing Mail List. To subscribe, your customers, or potential customers, send an e-mail message to the list server that says SUBSCRIBE FISH LIST. From then on they receive e-mail messages about fishing. And, if they want to post a message to the list server — perhaps about a great lake for fishing — they send a message to the server, and it automatically forwards it to everyone on the list. If you want to control the messages being sent to the subscribers, you can set up a moderated list. As the administrator of the list, you review the contents of each message posted to the server, and only forward those you consider appropriate.

List servers are a great marketing tool because the subscriber has asked to join the group. Unlike an unsolicited e-mail message, any message from the list server is welcome. I subscribe to two list servers — one from Statistics Canada, and one called The Laugh of The Day. Every day I get the latest statistics on the country and a few good jokes delivered right to my e-mail box.

Keep this tip in mind: If you decide to set up a business list server, try to keep the number of messages transmitted to a minimum. If a subscriber starts receiving more messages than they can read, they may send you an UNSUBSCRIBE message. I belonged to a mailing list about public relations and started receiving 50 messages a day. It was filling up my e-mail box and getting in the way of doing business. I unsubscribed even though a lot of the information was very interesting and useful. For this reason, I suggest you set up a moderated list server and control the quality and the quantity of the messages posted.

C. The World Wide Web: If you're reading this book, it's my bet you probably already have a Web site, or you're thinking about setting one up. Before I suggest some ways to make your Web site an effective marketing tool, I will briefly explain the technical features of the World Wide Web.

The World Wide Web is a communications platform that operates over the Internet. (A World Wide Web site is sometimes referred to as a Home Page, when actually a Home Page is the first screen visitors see when they come to your site.) They get to your site by typing in your Universal Resource Locator (URL), or what is more commonly referred to as your Web address. This address looks something like *www.biginc.on.ca*. When a visitor's browser (the software program used to access the World Wide Web) locates the computer your site is on, the digital files which make up your site are transmitted over the Internet to their computer. When a Web page appears on the screen, it contains graphics, text known as hyperlinks, and regular text. Visitors view the page's contents and can click on the hyperlinks to go to another page on your site or to another Web site altogether.

To create a Web site you need to write the copy and gather up the digital pictures and graphics. The site is designed in HyperText Markup Language (HTML), a rather primitive type of programming. Once the site is designed, it's placed on a Web server which can be accessed by anyone on the Internet who has a Web browser (unless you choose to restrict access). This server can be located in your office, in someone else's office (or home), or at an Internet service provider (ISP).

If your site is located at an ISP, you will pay a monthly fee for maintaining the site (data storage and transfer). The fee is based on the number and size of the digital files you place on the server (the more bits, the higher the cost), and on the number of files accessed and downloaded from your site by visitors.

If you're choosing an ISP to store your Web site, don't base your decision strictly on price. A low-cost supplier might have slower equipment and inadequate data lines. This can severely diminish access to your site.

From a marketing point of view, the key thing to remember about the Web is it is a nonintrusive medium. To see your site, people have to seek it out. It's not like a television ad that pops up during a football game or a billboard that suddenly comes into view on the highway. If someone doesn't want to see your site, you can't force it on them. You have to somehow make your site attractive enough so people will seek it out on their own. In general, if you take the advertising approach and put your brochure online, people are going to stay away. But if you put some entertaining, interesting, and useful information on the Web, your customers and prospects will keep coming back. Here are a few hints on how to make your Web site a powerful marketing tool.

- **Make it useful**: As I discussed earlier in the book, the major courier companies have created Web sites on which you can order a pickup, track the status of your parcel, and review your account. Major banks and trust companies have established online banking. PaymentLink Corporation offers PayLink, an online bill payment service.

  All of these sites are popular because they help one perform a function faster and easier than traditional methods. So instead of simply putting your brochure online, think of a function that could be performed electronically by your customers. If you're a retailer with a lot of repeat business, allow your customers to browse your merchandise and make purchases online. If you are a manufacturer or distributor, allow your customers to design their own products online or to browse through your warehouse inventory. If you have a law firm, let your clients create their own will or contract. If you run a restaurant, let your customers design their own menu and present it to them when they arrive at your restaurant. The menu can be printed on a color laser printer and include personal information about the guest of honor. If you own an art gallery, let your customers create their own art online and frame it for them. The key is to give customers the power to do it themselves.

- **Think public relations, not advertising**: Instead of putting your advertisement online, provide a valuable public service instead. If you're in the travel business, run a site offering tips about travel in foreign countries. If you're a waste disposal company, feature advice on how to dispose of dangerous chemicals. If you're a scuba diving company, provide a complete guide to all the scuba diving locations in the Caribbean. Before you put up your Web site, think about the subject matter you're an expert in, and build your site around it. The result will be greater interest in your site, and more repeat visitors.

- **Be entertaining**: Molson Breweries has a Web site called SoundBox which is all about rock music. You can download audio clips of popular rock bands, get concert listings, and read record and concert reviews. You can also join in Pub Chat and talk electronically to other people about music. To encourage people to return time and time again, the site is updated regularly.

  Although you might not have the resources of a major brewery, you can still be creative. Hire a comedy writer to post jokes regularly to your site. Or better yet, run a contest for the best jokes. Have your visitors contribute their favorite one-liners. Let them build up the content for you.
- **Use nonpartisan information**: Your Web site can provide a valuable service to your customers by offering nonpartisan information about every facet of your industry. If you're in the hospitality business, offer a list of all the hotels and restaurants in your market, even those of your competitors. If you run a camp trying to recruit campers, provide a list of all the camps, and links to their sites. If you're an automotive company, set up a site with a search function that allows your visitors to type in their needs and get a report on all the cars that meet those requirements — not just the cars you make. This might sound like giving the house away, but think about it; if you set up a nonpartisan site and give out valuable information, people will keep coming back. Your site will be the first place they go to when they want information about hotels, camps, or automobiles. And, because you control the content of the site, the person will see your products and services every time they access the site.
- **Make it interactive**: Consider adding a function to your site to give visitors instant feedback. Using JAVA scripting, you can offer you visitors an online software program. For

example, we work with a company that produces wireless transmission towers. Its clients and prospects are cellular and wireless service providers around the world, primarily the technicians at those companies. They have set up a site that helps technicians determine the exact number and placement of wireless towers for a given geographical area. The technician enters the specific parameters of the region and the program produces a topographical map detailing the ideal placement, power, and frequency of the wireless towers. This program is very useful to the company's clients and keeps them coming back again and again. In addition to JAVA programs, you can also provide database-driven content on your site. The users indicate what type of information they are looking for, and the program outputs a list from the database. You can also create a site that provides each user with a custom home page. Users decide what type of information they want to see on your site, and when they return the next time, the site greets each one as a repeat user.

- **Change the content regularly**: There is no greater sin on the World Wide Web than leaving your site alone and never changing it. If you want people to come to your site more than once or twice, you have to change the content regularly.

When you put up a Web site, think of yourself as a television producer. You need to provide new and stimulating content on a regular basis. You need to keep feeding the site with new information. You can't sit back and rest on your laurels. Having a Web site is like having your own television station.

Many companies launch a Web site and then find themselves ill-equipped to do the work needed to keep it interesting. Your company has to develop and commit to a long-term content strategy. If you find this daunting, you might consider getting your viewers to add content. Set up a way for visitors to post information and enlist people in your industry to provide content. They might be interested in doing the work if it provides them with valuable exposure.

- **Think locally**: When we think about the Internet, we usually think about global markets and international trade. But people live in local communities and most things they care about happen in their own neighborhood. So, if a lot of your business is local, consider sponsoring a Web site specifically for your community.
- **Include a survey form**: Every Web site should have a place for people to leave their name and e-mail address. You want to find out as much as you can about each visitor. To encourage them to leave their name, give them an incentive. Hold a contest, or offer some other compensation for filling out the form. You can offer them a free mouse pad, or free software to download. Ask if they want to join your e-mail list and receive regular information about your Web site's subject area.
- **Give visitors a digital present**: Give your Web visitors a digital present before they leave your site. This could be a screen saver, a software program, a computer game, or any other small promotion item.

  The Tourist Bureau of British Columbia hit the jackpot recently when it created a screen saver about its beautiful province. Once installed it displays gorgeous pictures of BC on your monitor whenever your computer sits idle. The BC screen saver was so well done that people began sending it by e-mail to their friends. It spread across the Internet like wildfire.

  Another good example of a digital present is a *Toy Story* game distributed free by Disney through its Web site. You can play the game online, or download it to play when you're not online. The *Toy Story* game is populated with Buzz, Woody, and other characters from the movie, so it makes a great promotional piece. My son loves the game, and it keeps us interested in seeing the movie again. So try and think of something you can give your Web site visitors. It doesn't have to be elaborate, it just has to be useful or entertaining.
- **Keep it simple:** When you create your Home Page, access it with a 14.4 modem. If your site takes more than 30 seconds to

appear, it's too big. All too often, graphic designers get carried away and put too many elaborate graphics on the Home Page. The site looks great but it takes too long to download. Visitors tire of waiting for it to appear, and click to something else. And even more ominous, they won't come back. In addition, keep the text on each page to a minimum. Web surfers prefer to click from page to page rather than scroll down. Break your site up into many small pages, rather than a few long ones.

D. Search engines: Once your Web site is online, you'll want to tell the Internet community. The first step is to list it with all the major search engines such as Yahoo, Excite, and Lycos. When people are looking for something on the Web, they most often go to one of these and perform a search for key words or concepts. Search engines present a list of sites matching the request. Visitors click on the sites that look most promising and through the hyperlink, are instantly taken there. It's really quite remarkable.

To be included in a search engine, you post your site address and a brief description containing as many relative key words or concepts as possible. In most cases search engines list your site for free, while others charge for enhanced services such as display ads.

Tip: When you're posting your site, make sure to include all the possible key words people might use if they're looking for you. For example, if you're in the landscaping business, your description might read "landscaping, tree planting, tree removal, gardening, outdoor renovation, driveway repair, autosprinklers." Instead of posting a flowery description of your business, put in as many key words as possible to increase the chances your site will appear when someone does a search.

E. Links from popular sites: To generate traffic on your site, consider paying to advertise on one of the popular Internet sites such as the Netscape Home Page, or on one of the major search engines. For example, if you place an ad on Yahoo, it will appear on thousands of

Web users' screens daily as they access the search engine. If they're interested, they just have to click on the ad to go to your site.

An ad on a major Internet site will increase the traffic to your site tremendously, but the cost might be prohibitive. In this case, it may be more appropriate to place your Web ad on a site that pertains specifically to your business. For example, if you charter sail boats, you might want to place your ad on the *Yachting World* site. This is a much more focused strategy because you know people who access the *Yachting World* site are interested in sailing.

F. Strategic Web partners: If you don't want to spend any money, you can try to arrange reciprocal links from related sites. You can offer to place a link on your site to someone else's site, if they create a link to your site. Strategic Web partnerships are a great idea because they will build traffic to your site and cost you virtually nothing.

G. Online shopping: A number of companies claim great success selling their products over the World Wide Web. Although no Internet merchant can say they've sold more than $1 million of merchandise on the Web, a number of smaller companies have made relatively large gains in revenue by going online. Virtual Vinelands of Los Altos in California sells its specialty wines over the Web and has reported monthly sales in the tens of thousands of dollars. Hot Hot Hot, a California purveyor of specialty hot sauces reports sales in excess of $60,000. These companies have profited from their online store because of their small size. Sales of $60,000 wouldn't get a major corporation very excited, but it can double sales for a smaller company almost overnight. At this time, setting up a shopping Web site is ideally suited for smaller companies who sell specialty products and don't have established retail distribution networks.

H. Newsgroups: If you want to get exposure in the Internet community, you can participate in the newsgroups. They are e-mail-based discussion groups on thousands of specific topics. People post e-mail messages to the group, or respond to those posted by other people. At last count, there were over 20,000 newsgroups about everything from knitting to nuclear physics.

You can search the list of newsgroups to see if there are any related to your line of business. For example, if you're in the commodities business, you can join *biz.commodities* and participate in the discussion by asking questions and offering advice. Blatant advertising in a newsgroup is taboo and not effective. You want to be seen as a person who contributes useful information to the group, not just someone trying to flog his wares. In this sense, participating in newsgroups is very much like traditional public relations.

I. File Transfer Protocol (FTP) Sites: A File Transfer Protocol (FTP) site is a place you can go to on the Internet and get digital computer files. There are no graphics or text, just a list of files to download. Although FTP isn't as visually exciting as the World Wide Web, it does have marketing applications. For instance, if you are a software company, you can set up an FTP site with all your technical documents, software upgrades, and utilities. By assigning passwords you can limit access to only your customers. They would appreciate the service because it makes it easier to get the software and documentation they need. If you have a lot of digital files and want to make them available to people on the Internet, or to a select group, consider setting up a FTP site.

Bulletin Board Service (BBS): When the World Wide Web came on the scene, some pundits predicted the end of Bulletin Board Services (BBS). They said the Web was the only viable online platform. BBS systems, they said, were a thing of the past. I disagree. In my opinion, BBS systems are set to surge in popularity as more and more people get online and begin to realize the limitations of the World Wide Web. Saying there is only one viable online platform is like saying you don't need newspapers because you have magazines. Or you don't need a radio because you have a television. A BBS is just one more online platform which could be more appropriate than a Web site for your purposes.

- **Choosing between BBS and Web**: A BBS is different from a Web site in one fundamental way: As a rule, a Web site is something you look at, while a BBS is something you participate in. If you're interested in getting people together to interact as a group, a BBS is more appropriate than a Web site. For example, I belong to the Mac Users Group BBS in Toronto. I connect to the BBS using my modem through regular telephone lines. The BBS has a number of different folders or conferences on various topics such as General News, Apple Update, Games, Graphic Design, Apple Utilities, and a number of discussion groups which I can participate in. The Mac BBS is a place I can go to get advice on how to get the most out of my computer. I know there are other people there who share the same interests and problems I have. If I need an answer to a technical question, I post it to the board and someone will read it and have the answer. Unlike a Web site, I can add content at any time by sending a message to a particular conference. Everyone else who subscribes to the BBS can see the message and respond to it. Because it is a place to congregate and discuss shared interests, the Mac BBS is like an electronic community.

  My company has created a number of different BBS systems for groups and organizations to help create an online community.

- *Metro Board Online* (MBO) is a BBS for members of the Board of Trade of Metropolitan Toronto. Members log on to find out what's happening at the Board, and participate in discussion groups about taxes, import/export opportunities, and a host of other business-related subjects.
- *BarterPlus Online* is a BBS for members of BarterPlus, the largest barter network in Canada. Members log in to see if there are any hot deals available on barter, to advertise their services, and to post messages about products and services they have for sale on barter.
- *Masthead Online* is a BBS for readers of *Masthead Magazine*, a publication for Canadian magazine publishers. The BBS

brings publishers together to discuss issues related to magazine publishing and offers industry suppliers an alternative method of reaching their market.

Each of these bulletin boards cater to well-defined groups. They provide an easy way for people with a similar interest to meet and share information. Unlike a Web site, the members of the BBS provide most of the content by posting messages. As the administer of the BBS, you are responsible for establishing the structure of the system and for setting up user accounts. From a marketing standpoint, a BBS has many important marketing features:

- **A BBS can be accessed through regular telephone lines.** When you conduct your digital communications audit, you may find most of your customers have a modem but not an Internet account. If you set up a Web site, they will not be able to access it. With a BBS they can access it through their telephone lines.
- **A BBS can be accessed through the Internet.** If most of your customers have an Internet account, they can log into the BBS through the Internet. Your BBS becomes a private Internet platform only available to your subscribers.
- **A BBS can be accessed through both the Internet and regular telephone lines.** Your subscribers can dial in through their Internet account or through regular telephone lines. Either way, they have access to your BBS. This is not possible with a Web site. If all your customers have a modem, and a few have an Internet account, this is an important consideration.
- **A BBS can be promoted as a unique product.** Let's say you set up Bonsai Online for your local bonsai tree club. When someone subscribes, you send them the Bonsai Online installation package which includes a software disk. When they install the software, the Bonsai Online logo appears on their screen. They click on "login," and dial up the BBS. While

they're online, the Bonsai Online logo stays on their screen the whole time. Unlike a Web site, which is just one in a few million, the packaging of a BBS gives it the quality of a distinct product and service.

- **A BBS is easy to administer.** Unlike a Web site, you do not need to constantly add content to the BBS. If you establish a core group of active users, they will generate the content and make the BBS interesting. As well, if you need to upload content, you simply send an e-mail message. You don't need to go through the laborious process of uploading an HTML document using FTP to your Web server. In fact, you can have dozens of people uploading content from their homes or businesses. You can't do that with a Web site.
- **A BBS can serve as your internal e-mail system.** In my company, my customer BBS also runs as our internal e-mail system. All my clients, suppliers, and associates are connected to it. When a client sends me an e-mail message, it appears instantly on my computer. It's as if we are all working in the same office using a network of computers which brings me closer to my clients.
- **A BBS is a proactive digital marketing tool**. If you want to get closer to your customers, you can proactively connect them to your BBS. For example, you might have 50 key customers; you schedule a visit to their office to hook them up to your BBS. If they don't have a modem, you buy them one. In a short time you can have all your key clients tied directly to your business electronically. This will improve efficiency and bring you closer to them. This proactive strategy works well for any service or consulting company and virtually any business-to-business organization.

If you want to set up a BBS, you have two options: set up the hardware and software in your office, or hire a BBS service bureau. (If you hire a service bureau, your costs will be significantly less, but you won't be able to integrate the BBS with your internal e-mail system.)

Get the ball rolling: To generate interest in your BBS, you need a lot of active subscribers. At first, you may want to give away the subscriptions for free. Once two or three hundred people are online, you can consider charging a fee. At first you may need to actively encourage people to post messages. Consider enlisting a core group of 20 people to act as facilitators; their job will be to get the ball rolling and once you reach a critical mass, the BBS will take on a life of its own.

Commercial online services: If you want to get involved with a commercial online service, such as America Online or the Microsoft Network, make sure the service's subscribers match your target market. These services are like huge Bulletin Board Services with thousands of subscribers. You can sponsor a conference or set up an online store. Marketing on a commercial service is akin to advertising on television or radio: you pay the service to gain access to its viewers/listeners (subscribers). The cost of advertising on commercial online services is comparable to magazine ad rates.

Some associations use commercial services as their version of a BBS. For most this is a mistake. For example, I belong to an association which has put its network on CompuServe. In order to access it, I have to get a subscription to CompuServe and pay them $10 a month plus online charges. Well, I'm not going to do it, and I'm sure most of the other members won't either. So you have a situation where most of your members can't, or won't, access your BBS network. It would be much better for the organization to set up their own BBS. It would be cheaper, too.

My advice for associations on commercial online services is: Set up your own Web site or BBS — preferably a BBS. If you want to promote yourself to a large group of subscribers, and you're willing to pay for it, then CompuServe or Prodigy may be a good idea. But don't use it to promote yourself to your established audience. It won't work.

Proprietary Internet platforms: If you have the resources, establish your own Internet platform. Get a team of programmers to develop a brand-new online system for the Internet. Build in all the features and capabilities that meet your needs, rather than trying to get a Web site to do it.

An example of a proprietary Internet platform is the Pointcast Network (PCN). As I explained, PCN uses PUSH technology to send information to your computer. Instead of accessing a Web site and looking at it one page at a time, the PCN sends you bits and bytes on an ongoing basis. In other words, the PCN broadcasts it, or pointcasts it, over the Internet to you every few minutes. The digital files sit on your hard drive so you can look at the content even if you're disconnected from the Internet. It's a terrific idea and one that is bound to take off because it gets around the bandwidth problem (see Chapter 4). Instead of waiting for files to download from a Web site, PCN sends all the data to you in large bursts. It's like a newspaper delivered to your door in the morning. Because all the digital information sits on your hard drive, you end up with a much faster, more interactive online event.

So think about building your own Internet platform such as an online ordering system, or a virtual reality tour of your store. Remember, anything is possible. You don't have to settle for the World Wide Web or one of the standard BBS platforms. You can do your own thing.

Cable networks: Although interactive television is still a few years away, cable networks are experimenting with some interactivity. Le Groupe Vidéotron Ltée, a leader in interactive cable television, recently teamed up with Kelloggs in Britain to produce an interactive commercial for children. When the commercial comes on, the child is able to click on icons on the screen and access additional content about Frosted Flakes.

If you are interested in piloting one of the early interactive commercials, speak to cable companies. Although you will be breaking new territory, there will be a lot of media exposure given to marketers who pioneer interactive television commercials; which in itself may make such a venture worthwhile.

In-store kiosks: Many retailers have experimented with kiosks and the public seem to like them. But kiosks have one major drawback: it takes a lot of time and money. One interactive kiosk can cost more than $100,000. But there is a solution. Why not set up a computer in your store and develop World Wide Web content for it? If you only have one store, the Web content only has to sit on the local hard drive. If you have more than one store, they can all be linked through the Internet (which makes system-wide content updates easy). The cost of each computer would only be about $5,000 (with all the multimedia bells and whistles), a far cry from a $100,000. And because Web pages are easy to navigate, users probably won't require any assistance. If you plan to set up interactive kiosks, keep these points in mind:

- **Set up an interactive survey**: Once again, get some information from the people who use your kiosk. Do they want to get on your mailing list? Would they like to receive information by e-mail? Do they use your competitor's products. What is their income level? Get the information and put it in your customer database.
- **Provide useful information**: If you own a cosmetic store, set up a kiosk that provides advice on health and beauty. If you run a restaurant, set up a kiosk in your lounge featuring an interactive contest or survey. If you operate a book store, provide a searchable database of all your books, along with reviews that can be printed out and taken home.
- **Put kiosks in places where people have to wait**: If you're a toothpaste company, why not set up kiosks in a medical and dental building, or in dentists' waiting areas. Kids can play interactive games which teach them about dental care. If you run a pharmacy, set up a kiosk about medications for customers to use while they wait for prescriptions.

If you thought a kiosk is beyond your budget, or too complex to administer, think about using a PC or Macintosh with Web software. You can create exciting, interactive content and make it available in your stores, and on the Internet at the same time.

Airline in-flight entertainment systems: British Airways was the first airline to create an interactive in-flight entertainment system. Passengers use handheld controllers to click through information shown on screens on the backs of the seats. They can play games, buy products, and send e-mail messages. If you were the marketing director for a tourist board or a hotel chain, you could create content for one of these services. In addition to British Airways, several other airlines are now offering this type of in-flight entertainment system.

MULTIMEDIA TOOLS

CD-ROM: You can create a multimedia presentation and send it out to your customers and prospects on CD-ROM. But be careful. Recently a friend of mine received a CD-ROM from an automotive company promoting its line of cars. He loaded in the software and ran the program. His screen froze and then all the other computers on his network crashed. It was a fiasco. Needless to say, he was not impressed, and won't be buying his fleet of company cars from them. The software was just too complex for his system. Having software that is too complex for a company's system is one major problem with commercial CD-ROMs. More than 30 percent of them are returned to the store because the customer's computer isn't powerful enough to handle it. Make sure your CD-ROM has been thoroughly debugged before you mail it out.

The advantage of a CD-ROM is its storage capacity. As discussed in Chapter 4, a CD-ROM can hold 640 megabytes of digital information. That's about the same as 500 floppy disks. Instead of producing an elaborate multimedia show that might crash everyone's computer, take advantage of CD storage capacity and produce a reference library instead. If you run a travel agency, create a CD-ROM featuring every resort in the world. If you're promoting a building supplies company, put your parts catalogue on a CD-ROM and give it to your customers. If you run a recruitment agency, create a CD-ROM featuring all your eligible employees. If you are trying to attract students to your university, send out a CD-ROM featuring all your courses and professors.

The more information you can cram onto the disk the better. Once again, instead of sending out self-serving advertising in a digital form, provide a useful service related to your line of business.

CD-ROM and online services: You can create a catalogue on CD-ROM and link it to an online service. For example, as a women's clothing manufacturer, you can create a CD-ROM containing all your current fashions and send it out to your retail buyers. The buyers can look through the catalogue and then log into your online service to check on the availability of the items they want and then place the order electronically. This idea can be used by any company which normally provides some sort of catalogue or has a long line of merchandise. Combining CD-ROMs and an online service also gets around the bandwidth problem: you can place elaborate graphics and video on the disk that would take too long to download from a Web site.

Floppy disks: You can send out a small digital file on a floppy disk as a promotion. While not everyone who has a computer has a CD-ROM drive, all have a floppy disk drive. However, there's no guarantee people are going to take the time to load the file onto their computer and watch it. You have to give them a good reason to look at it. To do this, why not put the answer to a mystery on the disk? Or create a small application which the recipient has to complete in order to win a prize? If you just stick your brochure on the disk, it's going to end up in the garbage.

Video game cartridges: More than 25 million households in Canada and the United States own at least one video game player. Why not create a digital promotion and send it out on a video game cartridge? You could use this idea to reach kids who play video games, or to reach adults who could ask their kids how to use it. The novelty of this idea would catch people's attention. Note: Check with the video game manufacturers regarding licensing rights.

FAX TOOLS

It took almost no time at all for the fax machine to become an indispensable tool for business. In addition to regular fax machines, fax modems have become increasingly popular. Using fax software, you can automatically send hundreds, even thousands, of faxes. This technology has led to "junk faxes" and has placed broadcast faxing in the role of marketing villain. But used properly, fax technology can be a very effective digital marketing tool because there is a very large installed base of fax machines.

Fax broadcast: Don't send out junk faxes to thousands of people unless you want to get a lot of nasty calls. I've tried this process a few times and received a lot of negative feedback. Instead, when you create your customer database, ask people if they want to receive information from you by fax. If they say yes, put their fax number in your fax broadcast list and send them a regular fax newsletter. If they ask to receive it, they won't consider it to be junk. Remember, you can also segment your fax numbers into groups which correspond to your market segments.

Fax-on-demand: You can set up a fax-on-demand server in your company to distribute information quickly and easily by fax to your customers and prospects. The customer, who has received a directory of the documents available, calls the system and a voice says: "Thank you for calling the Bonsai Lovers Fax-On-Demand System. Please enter your fax number now. Please enter the codes of the documents you wish to receive. Thank you. Your requested documents will be faxed to you in a few minutes." The fax-on-demand system handles the entire process.

BarterPlus Systems of Toronto, for example, uses fax-on-demand to provide information about its members. If you want to find out what restaurants are currently trading, you call up the system and enter the code for restaurants. Within minutes you receive a list of the restaurants by fax. It's amazingly fast and can be accessed 24 hours a day, seven days a week.

If you want to use a fax-on-demand system as a marketing tool, create a directory of the available documents and distribute it to your customers. The directory could include a list of restaurants, technical documents, bonsai trees, resorts, auto parts or anything else related to your business. If the information is useful and important to your customers or prospects, they will use this system. Fax-on-demand is most appropriate for business-to-business applications because most fax machines are located in offices.

Fax mailboxes: Like the voice mailboxes idea, you can create fax mailboxes for your best customers. You ask them what type of information they want and place documents in their fax box. They can access the box at any time to get the faxes sent to them. This puts the onus on the customer to request the documents, which raises the value of the service in their eyes. For example, let's pretend you're a human resources consultant. You can gather up articles and reports of interest to a specific client. You give her the number of the fax mailbox, and tell her she can access it at any time. If she does, she will be much more interested in reading the material than if you send it to her unsolicited.

Don't forget about the fax technology when devising your digital marketing strategy. If you are trying to reach a business market, fax may be your best choice; almost every business has a fax machine. You can send out a print directory or place an ad in a magazine or newspaper listing all the documents available. Structured properly, a fax-on-demand promotion can generate a lot of interest in your marketplace.

OTHER DIGITAL TOOLS

Proprietary software: You can create your own software program to help your customers and prospects do something faster and easier. The discount brokerage service of the Royal Bank of Canada, for example, has created a software program called *Action Direct*.

The program contains a list of more than 500 mutual funds, and shows you how to analyze the risk/return relationship for 16 different kinds of securities.

Electronic forms: If you use forms to deal with customers, think about creating electronic forms instead of paper forms. The Toronto Dominion Bank, for example, uses an electronic form for small business loan applications. To apply for a loan, you receive a disk containing an electronic form. You run it on your computer (no additional software is required) and fill in the fields. You can't close and submit the form unless you have correctly filled out all the fields. You simply return the disk to the bank and wait for the verdict. The electronic form is an excellent marketing tool for the bank; it sets it apart from its competition. The form is also less tedious to fill out than a printed form. When the bank receives the form, the computer quickly compiles and assesses it. As well, the computer enters the applications into a database to provide statistical profiles of the small business community.

Electronic forms are an easy way to create an online ordering system. Instead of building a sophisticated Web site with electronic ordering capabilities, simply make your order forms available in an electronic form. Any time customers want to place an order, they call up your order form template on their computer, fill it in, and send it to you by e-mail. When the order has been processed, you send confirmation by e-mail. One advantage of electronic order forms instead of a Web site ordering system is accessibility. An electronic order form can be filled in offline, and then sent out over e-mail. The customers don't have to log on to the Web to order. They don't even need a full Internet account. They just need to have e-mail capabilities.

Inexpensive software is available to create electronic forms and the process is relatively simple. Keep in mind that electronic forms can be distributed on disk, or made available on a BBS, a Web site, or by e-mail.

Pagers: If you have a small group of important clients, why not give each of them a pager, and regularly send them useful information over the pager network. You can lease annual pager accounts for less than $100 and get a discount if you buy in volume. A real estate company, for example, might give a pager to people who are looking for a house. When a house comes on the market, the pager will go off and give them information about the house. A pager service is an excellent idea for any company providing just-in-time services.

Virtual reality arcade machines: As a special promotion, you can lease a virtual reality (VR) arcade machine and send it across the country on a roadshow. You can create a custom VR program which includes graphics and environments related to your business. Because it delivers such a novel experience, your VR promotion would create lineups wherever it appears. As the price of the equipment falls, and the technology improves, virtual reality will become standard in retail environments (replacing kiosks), and eventually in your home.

COMING SOON

Digital Videodisk (DVD): As I explained in Chapter 4, DVD is the new enhanced CD-ROM format that holds many times more digital information on the same size disk. DVD allows you to create multimedia promotional tools with full screen video and libraries of reference data.

Wireless Personal Digital Assistants (PDA): When Apple introduced the Newton a few years ago, the personal digital assistant was born. Unfortunately, the first version of the Newton did not live up to expectations, but PDAs are not going away. In the next ten years, I predict PDAs with wireless access to online information services will become commonplace. In the United States, Sony has introduced its Magic Link PDA with wireless fax and e-mail capabilities. As these PDAs become more affordable, and the services connected to them become more ubiquitous, many marketing opportunities will present themselves. I foresee the day when you will be able to order a taxi or make a restaurant reservation, without using a phone, while standing on a street corner. Give it a few years.

Interactive television: Someday soon, your television is going to be interactive. On your television, you'll watch videos on demand or choose network shows from a selectable menu. While watching a "Seinfeld" rerun, you'll click on Jerry's box of cereal and look at a commercial for cornflakes. Of course, you'll also be able to search the World Wide Web, do banking, and order groceries to be delivered. Interactive television will be the revolution that unites the cyber-geeks and the couch potatoes.

Video-mail: When high bandwidth access to the Internet is available from cable or telephone companies, video-mail will become popular. In its first generation, you will take a digital video of yourself, and send it as an attachment to an e-mail message. Small black-and-white or color cameras which attach to your computer can be purchased for less than $150. Video-mail is possible today, but give it about five years to become really popular.

Virtual reality online: No digital format consumes more bandwidth than virtual reality. Until we have optical fiber connections directly wired into our homes, online virtual reality will be merely a dream. Give it about 20 years.

As I've discussed numerous times in this book, all these tools are simply that — tools. Only choose a digital marketing tool if it fits into your strategy. Remember, technology should be the servant, not the master of your business.

Now that I've discussed the digital marketing tools at your disposal, I will discuss the creative side of your digital marketing program.

What promotional ideas will attract the attention of your customers and prospects? How can you get people to use digital communications devices to learn more about your company and its products and services? Is there something you can do to proactively integrate your customers with your company in order to fight off competitors? To discover answers to these questions, read on and find out in Chapter 9 — Dream Up Your Digital Promotion.

CHAPTER 9

DREAM UP YOUR DIGITAL PROMOTION

I know this sounds crazy, but ever since yesterday, on the road, I've been seeing this shape. In shaving cream. Pillows. This means something. This is important...

Roy (Richard Dreyfuss) in
Close Encounters of the Third Kind, 1977

Steven Spielberg's film *Close Encounters of the Third Kind* provides an interesting metaphor for digital marketing. After witnessing several UFOs, the character played by Richard Dreyfuss becomes obsessed with the idea that aliens will land their spaceship on a mountain called Devil's Tower in Wyoming. His obsession is fanatical and nothing will stop him from getting to the mountain.

As a digital marketer, it's your job to dream up a promotional idea which will attract people to your Digital Domain. You must do something so exciting that your customers will seek you out using the telephone, the Internet, a BBS, or other digital media. You want them to become obsessed, just like Richard Dreyfuss. Even if you can't afford a huge spaceship, you can still dream up a great idea.

Creativity and strategic thinking can produce ideas that can attract the attention of the people in your market for years to come.

As I discussed in Chapter 2, digital marketing is fundamentally nonintrusive. Unlike traditional promotional media, such as a commercial that interrupts your TV show or a billboard that catches your eye on the highway, most promotions on digital media are seen only by people who voluntarily seek them out. A World Wide Web site, for example, is like a billboard on a back road; no one will see it unless they make a special effort. If your digital promotion is self-serving or simply an online version of your brochure, few people will be interested. You have to give them something in return such as a financial reward, useful information or something really entertaining.

Alternatively, you can use digital and online technology to proactively integrate your customers with your organization. You can create a private online network connecting all your customers, suppliers, and employees. You can add in special software programs and online order forms to help your clients deal with you faster and more efficiently. As well, you can develop an industry-wide online system which features content about everyone and everything in your industry — including information about your competitors. As I've noted, American Airlines adopted this strategy with its Sabre system. Even the smallest company can use this kind of proactive approach.

The purpose of this chapter is to get your mind working and your creative juices flowing. To help you come up with ideas for your digital strategy, I'll explain some basic principles and offer some hypothetical scenarios for different types of digital promotions.

DIGITAL ROADSIDE ATTRACTIONS

When you become a digital marketer, you also assume the role of Content Producer. It's your job to produce content for your digital promotion which is interesting, timely, useful, entertaining, and interactive. You have to plan ahead and be prepared to make content additions and revisions in order to provide real value. Remember, your customers and prospects don't want to read an electronic brochure; they want information that will help them or entertain them. They want an easier way to do something or a way to save or make money. You need to go beyond a traditional advertising mindset and produce content that will stimulate your customers and prospects, and bring them back again and again. Here are seven general types of digital promotions, along with suggested approaches for developing content.

1. Provide information people need. The digital age is also the information age. As computers become faster and online networks more pervasive, our society is producing greater and greater amounts of information. We're blessed with a wealth of facts and figures, but we're also suffering from information overload. The more information we have access to, the more overwhelmed we become. The problem of information overload is a major opportunity for marketers. You can gather and process information in ways that add value and meaning, or you can be the gatekeeper who points people to the information they're looking for.

The different ways to deliver these kinds of information services are:

A. General information: You can provide a useful service by gathering content on a particular subject and presenting it in a meaningful way. For example, a gardening company can gather information about gardening and create The Gardening BBS, Web site, and CD-ROM. People will seek out this information because it is entertaining and makes them better gardeners. You can sell this information or provide it free of charge in order to attract people to your company. This approach can be used for almost any subject matter related to your business.

B. Specialty information: If you have a small company and have limited time and money, you may need to narrow your focus and provide specialized information. If you only have one flower shop, for example, you can't compete against a large chain of shops because they have the money needed to gather all of the general information about gardening. You need to focus on a particular type of gardening subject such as "How to grow peonies," or become even more specialized: "How to grow white peonies." A motorcycle repair shop can focus on "How to overhaul the carburetor on a Harley Davidson." A dancing school might focus on "How to dance the tango," and a security company might provide specialized information on "Ways to protect your cottage from vandalism."

Not only will this strategy help you manage the time and the money required to maintain your digital promotion, but by focusing on a narrowly defined subject, you can develop your expertise and knowledge more thoroughly. Positioned properly, this expertise can help you stand out among the vast multitude of general information providers.

C. Information gatekeeper: Instead of gathering content and packaging it yourself, you can help people find the information they need by acting as an Information Gatekeeper. People will seek you out because you have done their looking for them. For example, you can create a Web site that acts as the gateway to all the information on the Internet about a particular subject. You can provide links to the sites on the Internet that you have reviewed and recommend.

For example, a pest control company might set up a Web site called PestLink which serves as the gateway to all the sites on the Internet about rats, mice, cockroaches, and other nasty critters. If they're judicious in choosing the sites and properly promote it, PestLink will be the first site people go to on the Internet when looking for information about pest control.

You will realize many advantages using the Information Gatekeeper strategy. You can provide a tremendous amount of information without having to produce it yourself, and it won't take a lot of the time to maintain.

D. Industry-wide information: Instead of providing information only about yourself, why not provide information about everyone and everything in your industry — including details about your competitors? Before you dismiss this idea as suicidal, think about it for a minute; if you provide all the information about an industry, where are people going to go first when they need to know something? Are they going to hunt through hundreds of different sources, or are they going to come to you first? They're going to come to you first. So why not try it? A manufacturer of helicopters, for example, can create a digital promotion called HeliNet to provide a comprehensive reference source on every type of helicopter on the market. If you're looking for a new whirlybird, you will go to HeliNet first because it provides all the information you need. If you run an art gallery, you can set up a Web site or a BBS listing and profiling all the art galleries in your city, or all the galleries in the world that specialize in your type of art. Your digital promotion will attract the attention of art lovers everywhere because you provide comprehensive, nonpartisan information.

The industry-wide information strategy has many advantages. By taking the high road, you can attract much more attention and interest than if you focus exclusively on your own company. You will also be able to control the content and appearance of the site in order to provide maximum exposure for your products and services. When your industry-wide service takes off, you can start charging your competitors to participate. All of a sudden, your competitors will be sending you cheques.

E. Targeted information: Instead of looking at content from a subject-oriented perspective, consider who you want to target and develop information of specific interest to them. For example, if you run a financial services company that helps retirees manage their money, you can gather seniors-oriented information related to their lifestyle and special needs. Information on travel, health, real estate, and entertainment can be made available on a Web site, a BBS, a 1-900 number, or an interactive voice-response system. Whenever seniors are using one of these services, they can choose to hear or see information about your financial services.

By providing targeted information for a particular group of people, you can become the leading information provider for their community. You can actually help create and define their community. This type of promotional strategy can provide your company with a tremendous amount of exposure.

F. Individualized information: You can develop information that is specially tailored for each person in your market. Using the profile in your customer database, you can create special messages for each individual based on his or her lifestyle and preferences. A car dealer, for example, can send out customized information based on the model of car a person drives, or based on how long they've owned the car. A record store can send out music reviews and music samples based on a person's musical tastes. A catering company can produce information on different foods based on the customer's stated preferences. This information can be distributed by e-mail, made available in a voice or fax mailbox, or placed on a personalized Web site.

By providing individualized information, you acknowledge the individual is unique and give the customers the type of information they want. This will increase their interest and raise the value of your company in their eyes. It will also give them the kind of background they need to make an educated buying decision.

G. Information-on-demand: You can develop a warehouse of information and allow your customers to put it together in ways most suited to their needs. A law firm, for example, can create a fax-on-demand service containing all the information anyone would need about legal matters. The firm can distribute a directory of all the documents contained on the system to their clients and prospects. A client can dial up the system and choose the information they want. The firm can make the same information available through a BBS or a Web site. In addition, a client can fill out a survey to request regular information on a number of different subjects.

This information can be faxed or e-mailed to her, or made available in a fax or voice mailbox. In both cases, the client gets to choose the information she wants to receive.

By providing an information-on-demand service, you don't have to second-guess your clients' needs. As well, additional marketing opportunities can be created if you compile a profile in your customer database about each person based on the type of information they've requested.

H. Just-in-time data: Sometimes you need to know something at the right time to act upon it. Knowing what horse is going to win is more useful before the race, than after. So why not provide your customers with just-in-time information? For example, a wholesaler can provide its best customers with beepers to alert them when products they want are available. The customer can send back an instant reply asking to have the merchandise held for one hour. A specialty food store can send out an e-mail message alerting its customers that fresh lobsters have just arrived from Maine and will be available for only the next three hours. Or a bakery can send out a fax message near the end of the day to help sell off the fresh baking it has left.

The Just-In-Time Information strategy works best with any business where a product or service is perishable — such as hotels, restaurants, airlines — or where transactions happen quickly — such as specialty, wholesale, and financial services.

I. Insider information: You can provide your best customers with information which is available only to them. By making it exclusive, you raise the value of the information in the eyes of the customers. For example, a grocery store chain can create a Web site or a BBS which contains exclusive recipes, coupons, entertainment ideas, and celebrity interviews. Only customers with a user identification number and a password can access the information. A camera store can create an exclusive site for its best customers with special deals on cameras and lenses, digital photographs from world-class photographers, and instructions on how to take better pictures. Once again, only customers with an ID and password can access it.

By creating a private, members-only club, you strengthen your relationship with your customers by making them feel special. As well, it encourages other customers and prospects to seek membership with you.

In each of these cases, an effort must be made to provide quality content and to change it on a continuous basis. If your information is perceived as stale, your customers and prospects will lose interest and move on. So once you make the decision to provide information, be prepared to update it regularly. The frequency of the changes depends on the subject matter and on the type of business you operate.

One final note on information content. Although it's preferable to provide dynamic information which is constantly changing, there is a purpose to putting simple product information on a Web site or on a fax or voice mail system. If you have a lot of product information, making it available electronically can save you time and money. If someone calls you long distance and requests information about your company, you can direct them to your Web site rather than sending them a package in the mail. Potential customers will receive your material quickly (as long as they're online), and you'll save the cost of printing and mailing a package. So there is a case for putting your brochure online, but try to go beyond such a basic strategy.

2. Make something faster or easier to do. If you give people a faster or easier way to do something, they'll be attracted to your digital promotion. For example, you might create an Odd Jobs Online service. A client can access your online order form and enter all the odd jobs she needs done such as shopping, repairs, deliveries, and cleaning. The computer will collate these requests along with hundreds of other client requests and determine the most efficient method to complete all the jobs. Within minutes the client will receive a quote for the jobs, who will handle them, and when they will be completed. If the quote is satisfactory, the client will click on the order button. If there is a problem with the quote, the client will change and resubmit the request. Employees of Odd Jobs Online will log into the system each Monday morning and receive a weekly schedule of jobs, outlining where to go and what to do.

Services that require a relatively complex transaction — such as ticket ordering, grocery shopping, academic course enrollment, and loan applications — can be handled over a computer or an interactive telephone system. As I mentioned in the last chapter, electronic order forms are an excellent digital tool because they help your customers deal with you faster and more easily.

3. Help people save money or make money. If you help people make or save money, they will be very attracted to your digital promotion. To help people save money, you might create a service called Price Point Online to provide the current price on all major consumer products and services at all major retailers in your city. Subscribers can access the system through a private BBS network, and enter the desired product in the database search engine. Within seconds, a report is displayed listing the current price for that product offered by local retailers. Subscribers can see instantly which retailer offers the best price. Of course, if the subscriber is interested in buying, they can click on the retailer's logo and go to their online shopping center. By using the service, the subscribers always know they're getting the lowest price. Of course, this service does not need to be limited to a local area; it can be worldwide. Instead of driving to the store to get the product, subscribers can receive merchandise by overnight delivery. As the creator of this service, you will make money from the subscribers and from the retailers who pay for display advertising.

To help people make money, you might create a service called Garage Sale Online. Customers who have a lot of furniture to get rid of can submit a list of items for the database. When people are looking for something, they enter their request in the search engine to see a list of the available items. If they find something they want, they contact the seller by e-mail or telephone and arrange the transaction.

Garage Sale Online can be made available on the World Wide Web, over the telephone, or using a fax-on-demand system. You can operate this network as a stand-alone company or use it to promote your existing services. Garage Sale Online would be a good promotional tool for a moving company.

4. Help people learn something. If you provide quality educational content, many people will seek out your digital promotion of their own free will. A classical music radio station, for example, can create a series of electronic courses on the history of classical music. Listeners can access the Web site and download the courses. Each course might teach them about a different classical composer; it can include audio clips, digital video clips, and links to other sites on the Internet about classical music. Of course, all the courses can be repackaged and sold on CD-ROM. You can also provide an interactive course accessed over the telephone.

Any company or organization which has something to teach people can adopt the educational approach. A hardware store can teach people about home repairs. A luggage or travel company can teach foreign languages. A Thai restaurant can teach Thai cooking. A catering company can teach entertaining skills. A boating company can teach nautical safety. In each case, the company can team up with someone who excels at teaching the subject matter. The educational content can be given away as a part of a promotional strategy or sold as a service.

5. Provide entertaining content. If you provide entertaining content, people will flock to your digital promotion. A family restaurant can create a fun software game for children to play, or provide a 1-800 number children can call to hear their favorite cartoon character tell a bedtime story. A bowling ball company can create a bowling program people can play on their computers. They can send e-mail files of scores to the company to win a new bowling ball or a trip to the Lithuanian Bowling Championships. A celebrity news magazine can broadcast daily e-mail gossip to its readers about their favorite Hollywood notables. To subscribe, a person fills out an electronic survey to indicate if she prefers news about celebrity marriages, celebrity divorces, or celebrity remarriages. You can hire a local comedian and produce hundreds of funny vignettes available by telephone. People can call up to get their daily laugh and hear a promotional message. You can team up with a cellular telephone company and offer a comedy show available free to cellular customers. The show can be supported by interactive advertising spots. The principle here is, if you leave them laughing, they will be sure to come back again.

6. Bring people together. If you bring your customers together in a digital setting, they will appreciate your social organizing efforts. A camera company, for instance, can create a BBS network for photography enthusiasts. People interested in photography can log into the system to exchange ideas, tips, and questions with other photophiles. As the organizer of the BBS, you can create different meeting areas (called conferences) which highlight a particular subject such as Beginner's Corner, Night Photography, Member Gallery, Lighting, Composition, and Professional Photography. In each conference, people can leave questions and reply to queries if they have an answer. You can also have a group of experts available to answer technical questions. In time, using your BBS will become an important part of their hobby. The social nature of the BBS will also put you in an excellent position to promote your products and services.

If you have a large potential audience of people who share the same interests, consider bringing them together electronically. A BBS is appropriate for a community because it's easy for everyone to contribute content. This community approach is appropriate, as well, for any type of association or club.

7. Do something never seen before. The first person to do something is always remembered because they get all the publicity. Do you know the second person who flew across the Atlantic after Charles Lindburgh? Do you know who introduced a line of photocopiers after Xerox? Not likely. So why not become the first to do something unique with digital technology? Be the first company in your industry to set up a BBS network, or be the first in your city to provide electronic coupons on a smart card. You can create a new platform on the Internet, or be the first to use a virtual reality machine to promote your products. The media will do stories about your pioneer efforts and the public will come running to your digital promotion to satisfy their curiosity and to see what all the fuss is about.

All the promotional ideas mentioned above are designed to attract attention to your company, to foster an ongoing relationship with your customers, and to bring new prospects into your sphere of influence. But this is just half the story. You can also take a proactive approach. You can take initiatives to integrate your customers more closely to your company and thereby strengthen your business relationships. I call these stratagems Proactive Digital Programs.

PROACTIVE DIGITAL PROGRAMS

1. Customer integration. When I developed my company's private BBS network in 1990, my goal was to further integrate my clients into my operation. I approached each client and got them online. If they didn't have a modem, I gave them one. If they didn't know how to use the BBS system, I took the time to teach them. It was time-consuming and costly, but it worked. Today, most of my clients are hardwired to my company. It's as if their computers are linked directly to the network in my office. If I need a client to review a news release, I send her the word processing document by e-mail. She makes her changes and sends it back to me. It's faster and easier, for the client and for me, than other methods. Together, we can get more done for less cost. In addition, all my associates and suppliers are connected to the system. When we lay out a newsletter or a brochure, we post the Pagemaker file to our BBS and the printer electronically accesses it. We don't have to send faxes or diskettes by courier. It all happens electronically.

No matter what size of company you work for or operate, you can take this proactive approach. Take a look at your customer base. What would happen if you created a private online network and took the effort to hook up all your customers? Would it be easier or harder to provide them with information? Would your relationship become closer or more distant? Would you be able to provide better or worse service? Would your postage, printing, and long-distance costs rise or fall? Indeed, the initial cost would be high in terms of both time and money, but in the long run, the benefits would be substantial.

If you're interested in integrating your customers with your operation, first conduct a digital communications audit. Find out their technical capabilities. If they're all on the Internet, set up a Web site which is only accessible by your customers. Add order forms, application forms, account records, and searchable databases. Take all the transactions which you normally conduct in person or over the telephone, and create an electronic, online counterpart.

2. Loyalty programs. Loyalty programs or best customer clubs are becoming very popular across North America. As a member of a loyalty program, you receive points every time you make a purchase. These points are calculated at the checkout counter and fed into a customer database. When you have accumulated enough points, you can redeem them for merchandise or services.

Many department chains, grocery stores, airlines, hotels, and car rental companies have introduced some form of loyalty program. The concept works best for companies that sell high-margin, premium-priced products which are purchased on an ongoing basis. However, even the smallest company can create some kind of loyalty program. If you run a bookstore, you can get your customers to sign up for a Preferred Customer Club. To join, customers fill out a survey indicating their favorite types of books and what other bookstores they frequent. Every time they buy a book at your store, they receive points, and once they reach a certain level, they get a book for free. In this way, you can gather information for your database and provide your customers with a reason to shop at your store rather than at your competitors'. A small loyalty program can be run with a single PC and an inexpensive database program. Tip: Give your customers an immediate incentive — such as a free bookmark or 15 percent off their purchase — for filling out an application form.

3. Market research programs. By speaking directly to your customers instead of talking to strangers, you can simultaneously conduct market research and build your customer database at the same time. Give them an incentive to participate in a survey; call up and offer them a $40 coupon if they'll answer 15 questions. Stop them in your store and ask them the questions.

Or you could conduct a survey of your entire industry. Put all the information into a database and release the findings in a report published in trade or business publications. You will be perceived as the expert in the industry, attract new customers, and be better able to maintain a value-added pricing strategy.

4. Digital cross-promotions. Why not join with other companies to create a digital cross-promotion? By sharing the development of the program, you can lower your up-front digital marketing costs or use the savings to fund additional activity. You can also share your existing resources. If your partner has a sophisticated voice mail system, you can trade it for your advanced Web site facilities. As well, a digital cross-promotion will provide you with leads and traffic generated by your partner's digital presence, and vice versa. Look for digital partners who cater to the same market as you but provide a totally different product or service.

5. Sales force programs. If you have a team of salespeople, give each one a laptop computer with customer tracking software. When visiting a customer or prospect, the salesperson can ask questions and enter the answers into the laptop. Each night, your sales team can connect their computers to your online network and upload the information right into your customer database. You can go one step further and provide your salespeople with just-in-time access to your company's information system through a cellular modem on their laptop. While they're meeting with a customer, the salesperson can check on inventory levels and immediately place orders. In a few years, handheld personal digital assistants (PDAs) will be advanced enough to provide this type of functionality.

6. Digital intermediary. You can set up an information network that controls the flow of information in your industry. For example, a forestry products company can establish an industry-wide system for sourcing lumber inventory levels. A buyer can enter the type of lumber he's looking for, and receive a report in seconds. He can immediately order the lumber or send back a request for a lower price. The buyer will use the system because it gives him access to all the information he needs to do his job quickly and easily. If the lumber company aggressively pursues this strategy and gets all the lumber buyers online, its competitors will have to join the system or go out of business. The system will become the way in which all lumber products are bought and sold throughout the world. This type of system can be developed in any industry where buyers spend a lot of time sourcing products and negotiating prices.

7. Public service and community programs. You can use digital technology to help your community. You can get involved in a local charity or provide computers to public schools, or create a Web site to support a worthy cause, or create an information database to help fight a disease. In each case, you will be doing a good deed and raising your profile in the community.

DIRECT DIGITAL SALES PROGRAMS

As of 1996, only a few companies have had success selling products on the Internet, but their success has encouraged many companies to set up virtual shopping centers. I believe online shopping works best with products which cannot be found in stores or in any other way. As more people come online and the cybermarket expands, you'll see products and services emerge which are sold only online. In the meantime, here are three ways to directly sell your products using digital and online technology:

1. Direct online shopping. If you have a product without traditional distribution channels, you might find a ready market on the Internet. The cost of setting up a Web online shopping store is very low compared to other distribution methods. This allows you to undercut your competitor's price or realize a greater margin for yourself. The trick is to promote the location of your online shopping site using the Internet search engines and cooperative hyperlinks from other Web sites. You can also advertise the location of your site in traditional media such as trade and consumer magazines, although this will increase your marketing costs. Direct online shopping works best with premium-priced products which can be delivered by courier, such as vintage wines, gourmet coffees, specialty foods, magazine subscriptions, software, eyewear, and athletic equipment. Direct online shopping is also effective for products which come in large inventories such as records, books, and videos. There is a site on the Internet, for example, called Musicnow which sells thousands of record titles through a searchable database. You can even click on a title and hear a sample of the recording.

2. Online shopping malls. Instead of going it alone with your own online store, you can link up with one of the many World Wide Web shopping malls. You can create your own Web site and pay for a link from the mall, or have the mall operators create a site for you. At this early stage in the development of the Internet, I question the marketing impact of general online shopping malls because the average person is not ready to buy online consumer products which they can get at the local grocery store or discount warehouses. The most successful online shopping malls will be those sites with a single product theme such as the Life Insurance Mall and the Bonsai Lovers' Mall, or those which cater to a certain segment of the population. Tip: If you want to sell your products on an Internet shopping mall, look around for the best deal. Instead of paying a monthly fee to the mall owners for promoting your products, offer them a piece of the action. As I discussed in Chapter 2, digital promotions should only be based on a results or commission basis. So pay the mall owners a commission on each item sold instead of a flat monthly fee.

3. In-store interactive shopping. If you want to expand the products offered in your store, you can set up an interactive shopping kiosk. Patrons will browse your in-store kiosk and if they see something they like, they will order it. You deliver it to them in a few days. An in-store kiosk allows you to offer a much larger selection of products than you could physically display in your store. It will also lower your overhead and generate consumer curiosity because of its novelty. As I explained in Chapter 8, your in-store kiosk can be placed online so your customers can check out your merchandise from home.

PUT IT ALL TOGETHER

These are just some of the strategies you can use to promote your company using online and digital technology. When you have reviewed each one and chosen the strategies most appropriate for your situation, you need to put all the pieces together into an integrated digital marketing program. Chapter 10 provides eight ideas for complete digital marketing programs.

CHAPTER 10

PUT ALL THE BITS AND BYTES TOGETHER

When all of us had done, Fowler Schocken touched another button and showed us a chart. He explained it carefully, item by item; he showed us tables and graphs and diagrams of the entire new department set up to handle the (marketing) of Venus. I envied the man who would head the Venus Section; any of us would have been proud to take the job.

The Space Merchants
Frederik Pohl/C.M. Kornbluth, 1952

When they wrote *The Space Merchants* in the early 1950s, the authors made fanciful predictions about the future of marketing. Advertising is beamed onto the windshields of flying cars. Subliminal messages are piped through the radio and television ads are projected right onto the retina of the eye. But in spite of their vivid imaginations, the authors failed to predict the emergence of digital marketing. They did not realize marketing in the 1990s would encompass such a rich and seemingly endless variety of possibilities.

To help you sort through these possibilities, I offer the following hypothetical digital marketing programs. They're based on the Strategic Digital Marketing Model and the digital marketing strategies presented in the previous chapter. I hope they assist you in developing your own digital marketing program.

THE INFORMATION PROVIDER

Big Bob's Hardware Emporium: With 475 stores, Big Bob's Hardware Emporium is one of the largest retailers of hardware and building supplies in North America. During the past three years, Big Bob's has developed an effective Information Provider digital marketing program.

Big Bob's has set up an Information Division to create educational material about home repairs and renovations. The Information Division has packaged and distributed information in both digital and traditional formats including CD-ROMs, online databases, a World Wide Web site, and a series of books and videotapes. They provide some material free of charge and they sell some at the retail level. The World Wide Web site, for example, is available for free and has become one of the most active sites on the Internet. Anyone looking for advice on "How to fix a leaky faucet" or "How to build a gazebo" turns first to Big Bob's site because they know the answer will be there.

As a provider of useful, high-quality information, Big Bob's attracts a lot of attention on the Internet from its customers and prospective customers. They ask people accessing the Web site to join Big Bob's Customer Club by filling out an online questionnaire. (For filling out the form, the person receives a free glove compartment tool kit.) With this information in its database, Big Bob's can send out regular e-mail messages containing renovation and repair tips to customers based on their stated information needs. As well, the biweekly e-mail messages contain electronic coupons and special offers redeemable at Big Bob's.

Customers who are not on the Internet can also join the Big Bob's Customer Club. By filling out a questionnaire at the store, they receive a Big Bob's Customer Card which they present every time they buy something at the store. They're asked if they would like to receive regular voice mail messages about home repairs, promotions, and special member discounts. If they agree, the database software compiles biweekly messages — based on the customers' stated preferences — and automatically dials up the customers. The message says: "If you would like to hear your personalized Big Bob's Hardware Show, press '2' on your telephone. If you would like to call back later to hear your personalized voice mail broadcast, dial 1-800-BIG-BOBS and enter the PIN number on your Customer Card." During the broadcast, customers are asked if they would like to receive coupons for various products. Every month, newsletters are sent to customers containing the exact coupons they requested.

In this way, Big Bob's Hardware Emporium fosters an ongoing relationship with its customers by providing them with useful and entertaining information. By focusing on the development of quality information, the company can take its content and roll it out in a number of different media including the Internet, the telephone, CD-ROMs, newsletters, books, and videos. If a new digital platform emerges, they will be able to take the content and distribute it in that way as well. In addition, the Information Division has become a profit center in its own right through the sales of CD-ROMs, books and videos. In fact, the published works are sold in bookstores as well as video stores.

THE DATABASE MARKETER

The Gourmet Baby Food Company: For five years, The Gourmet Baby Food Company has been very successful in marketing its line of high-end gourmet baby foods through direct mail. Parents who want their babies to develop a taste for the finer things in life have been ordering the products in record numbers. The company has decided to expand its line and convince even more parents to serve their babies strained duck à l'orange and mushy escargot au gratin. To achieve this goal, they have developed a strategic digital marketing program based on database marketing.

The first step is to send out a survey to all parents in Toledo, Ohio with children under three years old. (Toledo is the company's test market.) Each family receives a lengthy questionnaire that asks them all about their baby food buying habits and concerns. For completing the survey, the family is entered into a contest to win a university scholarship for their child, along with a coupon for $40 off a case of gourmet baby food. The contest and financial incentive pull in more than 45 percent of the surveyed families.

The company feeds all the returned data into the database. After analyzing the data, it segments its market into four different groups: Gourmet Lovers, Health Watchers, Knowledge Needers, and Not Interested. Unique promotional pieces are produced for, and distributed to, the first three segments. The Gourmet Lovers receive material which highlights the tasty gourmet ingredients and features full-color pictures of happy, gormandizing toddlers. The Health Watchers receive a catalogue emphasizing the healthy ingredients of the products along with a pediatrician's report on the nutritional value of gourmet foods. The Knowledge Needers receive material with extensive research data on the products. The results of this segmented campaign are very positive; each segment appreciates receiving the type of information they requested and place thousands of orders.

Following the test in Toledo, the company rolls out the program across North America. More than ten million families receive the questionnaire, and more than three million mail it in. As the size and complexity of the database grows, the company creates more than ten different segments and develops specific marketing promotions for each one.

With the initial campaign complete, the Gourmet Baby Food Company aggressively expands its database marketing program. It forms an alliance with a mailing list agency which will provide the names of all new mothers in North America. Four months after a child is born, the company sends the parents a generic catalogue along with the questionnaire, and places all the respondents into the database. To capture transactional data on people who won't fill out the survey, the company sends out a digital cheque to parents. The cheque is worth $5 off any brand of baby food found in a retail store. To endorse the cheque, the parent must fill out the short survey on the back and present it when making a purchase. Within days of the transaction, the company receives names and profiles on these people as well.

Within a few years, The Gourmet Baby Food Company has an extremely complex and valuable database. It knows exactly what types of customers it has in the marketplace; it knows what kinds of promotions work best for each of its market segments. In addition, the company has eliminated all intermediary distributors and promotional media, thereby increasing its margin and lowering its relative marketing costs.

THE PROACTIVE INTEGRATOR

Webbed Feet Film and Printing: As a medium-size printing company in Toronto, Webbed Feet Film and Printing decides to proactively integrate its customers with its operation. After conducting a digital communications audit, the company discovers 90 percent of its customers have a computer and modem. Based on this technological profile of its customer base, the company decides to develop a private online network (BBS) called Webbed Feet Worldwide.

Following three months of design and development, the BBS is ready. Webbed Feet salespeople call up each customer and make an appointment. At the customer's office, the salesperson installs the online software and shows the customer how to use it. The Network features a number of useful electronic forms to make it easy and simple for a customer to deal with Webbed Feet. If the customer needs a quote on a printing job, he fills in the online form. If he wants to send a layout file to Webbed Feet, he simply sends an e-mail message with the file(s) attached. There are also online forms to track the status of each job in progress, and a way to electronically pay invoices.

Within a few months, more than 250 customers are hardwired to the Webbed Feet plant. Quotes are being calculated and sent back to the clients in under an hour. Projects are being done in half the time previously required. The use of couriers has dropped substantially. Customer invoices are being paid an average of 15 days faster due to the online bill payment feature. As well, clients are using Webbed Feet more often than they use competitors because the online system makes switching back to a traditional printing system seem archaic and bothersome.

The key here is Webbed Feet's proactive approach. The company takes each client by the hand and installs the software for him. If the client doesn't have a modem, it supplies one. If a client needs to be coached on how to use the system, it takes the time to teach him.

If the company had taken a passive approach and simply set up a World Wide Web site and told its clients to use it, it would have taken years for everyone to get around to doing so. By that time, all of Webbed Feet's competitors would be on the bandwagon with their own version of the system. The competitive advantage would be lost.

In addition, the astute marketers at Webbed Feet have adopted a parallel strategy to corner their entire industry. They have developed a system on the World Wide Web called Inter-Quote, which people can use free of charge to get quotes from a variety of printers. When people need printing, they simply enter the specs for the project on an electronic form and click Submit. Printers who subscribe to the service, for a substantial annual fee, can take a look at the project and decide if they want to reply with a quote. Later, the customer returns to Inter-Quote and reviews a dozen or so quotes. Instead of spending days calling different printers, the customer gets a complete list of competitive quotes in a matter of hours.

By taking its knowledge of the printing industry and building this industry-wide quoting system, Webbed Feet has become more than just a printer among many; through Inter-Quote, it has become the information conduit for its entire industry, and has generated a substantial amount of revenue from its competitors.

THE DIGITAL COMMUNITY

International Association of Sperm Bank Operators: At their annual convention last year, the members of the International

Association of Sperm Bank Operators (IASBO) voted to create a private online network for their organization. While many of the members expressed an interest in a Web site, the more knowledgeable members convinced everyone to go with a BBS format. Nine months after it was first conceived, SpermNet was born.

SpermNet gives IASBO members around the world a way to electronically communicate with each other. Each member receives a private account with a password. Using the SpermNet software, the member dials up the system to send and retrieve e-mail, download policy papers, enter discussion groups, and most importantly, search the SpermNet database for eligible sperm donors.

To serve the different technological needs of its members, IASBO created three ways to access SpermNet: through regular telephone lines using a local number, through a toll-free 1-800 number, and through the Internet. The members pay an annual fee for access to the system and pay no online time charges.

As more members join SpermNet, the amount of content on the system grows exponentially. Each special committee of the association has its own conference, which is only accessible by members of that committee. Members are invited to upload any content they wish to share with other people. As well, all the association's archives have been stored on CD-ROM and are accessible through the BBS.

The SpermNet BBS has revitalized the fortunes of the association. Membership enrollment and attendance at monthly meetings has gone up. As well, the association is now able to provide more service and more information to more members at less cost. For example, its monthly newsletter is now distributed only on the BBS; it is converted into a portable document format (PDF) and sent to each member by e-mail. The member can download the file onto his computer and read the newsletter in full-color right on his screen. If he finds an article he wants to take home, he simply prints it off on his laser printer. As such, it's the member who is paying for the printing of the newsletter, not the association.

To attract new members, the association has also created a Web site which promotes SpermNet. The prospective member can download the BBS software and log in as a guest visitor. The visitor can see a lot of the available information, but has limited functionality. At the end of his tour, the visitor can fill out an online membership application.

In this way, the association has the best of both worlds: it has fostered an electronic community using the BBS, and it has created a powerful marketing tool on the World Wide Web. The two systems perform their unique functions to serve the objectives of the association.

THE SMART INNOVATOR

The Bowling Ball Alarm Agency: As I'm sure you've read in the newspapers, the rate of bowling ball theft has been rising steadily in recent years. Bowling balls have become a hot item on the black market as the sport grows in popularity among aging baby boomers. To combat the pilfering of bowling balls, an enterprising company called the Bowling Ball Alarm Agency has come to the rescue. It has invented the Smart Bowling Ball with an internal computer chip that identifies its owner. If the ball is lost or stolen, it can be located using the Global Positioning System (GPS). No matter where the ball is located in the world, it can be found and returned to its rightful owner. In addition to sales of its Smart Bowling Ball, the company provides its search and return service. Each customer must sign up for the service when they purchase the ball and pay an annual fee for complete bowling ball peace of mind.

In addition to its antitheft capabilities, the Smart Bowling Balls have a number of other digital capabilities. The balls can be used in automated Pay-As-You-Play Bowling Alleys which charge customers for each frame they play. Each time the Smart Ball is rolled, the alley identifies its owner and puts a charge on his or her credit card. The ball also keeps track of every time it is rolled and can provide a complete report on its playing history. The owner simply connects the ball to his computer to receive a complete printout using the Smart Bowling Bowl software.

Because of its novelty and obvious improvement over regular

bowling balls, the Smart Bowling Ball has received millions of dollars of free publicity around the world. Everyone is talking about them. The inventors of the Smart Bowling Ball have also received enquiries from hundreds of other companies who want to adapt their technology to other products and services. And by turning their seemingly ordinary product into a smart information device, the company has created almost unlimited opportunities for itself.

THE INTERACTIVE UNDERTAKER

Frederick's Funeral Homes: Business has been steady at the 200 Frederick's Funeral Homes across the country, but sales revenue per client has not grown as projected. Loved ones are not opting for the little extras such as mahogany caskets, horse-drawn carriages, fresh floral bouquets, live chamber music, and 21-gun salutes. Something has to be done to upsell mourners or the company's board of directors will face grave consequences.

Using the Strategic Digital Marketing Model, the marketing department decides to create an interactive sales environment aimed at the predeceased rather than mourners. They launch an advertising campaign with the theme, "If you want something done right, do it yourself." The campaign is designed to get people to preplan their funeral rather than give the responsibility to their less-than-generous relatives. To generate a high response, the ads offer a free urn to anyone who visits the Frederick's Interactive Funeral Planning Center.

At each center, the prospective customers sit in front of a touchscreen computer monitor. A video of Frank Frederick comes on the screen and explains the importance of preplanning their final farewell. At the end of Frederick's greeting, the prospects view a menu of different funeral packages, and for each package, see a video depicting exactly what kind of funeral they could have. They may "Select '1' for our Discount Service," or "Select '2' for our Deluxe, Spare-No-Expense State Funeral." Once they select the package they want, the customers can fine-tune the process. "Would you like brass or silver handles on your casket? Would you like one or two police squad cars leading the procession? Would you like a humanist service or a religious service?" Within an hour, the customer plans his funeral in complete privacy. In addition, he immediately receives the calculated bill. Customers can pay by cash, cheque, or credit card, or choose one of the three different lease-to-own programs.

Following the success of the interactive preplanning centers, Frederick's places the entire process on the Internet. Now people can plan their funerals from the comfort of their own home. In addition, Frederick's lists more than 400 different cemeteries on the system. (Each cemetery pays Frederick's $5,000 a year to list their available plots.) People can buy funeral plots online by simply clicking on an icon. As an additional service, people can search Frederick's database to find the burial location of their long-lost loved ones.

By "informationalizing" their business, Fredrick's has increased sales of its traditional offerings, and added a number of new and profitable information services.

THE DIGITAL COMMUNICATOR

Liability & Lawsuits: To attract new clients for Liability & Lawsuits, her one-woman law firm, Lillian Litigious has become the consummate digital communicator. To build awareness of her services, she uses a wide variety of digital tools including e-mail, newsgroups, the World Wide Web, interactive voice response, and fax-on-demand. She also provides her potential clients with a wealth of useful information.

Lillian spends her marketing time at her computer communicating with clients and potential clients. She has become an active member of four Internet newsgroups where she provides advice to anyone who is thinking about suing someone. She has created a Web site with a private chat room where Lillian conducts online consultations with potential clients. She has also set up a 1-800 number people can call to select from a variety of menu options: "Press '1' for whiplash, press '2' for small claims, press '3' for malpractice." The caller can either hear a voice message about these subjects, or have the information sent directly to his fax machine.

With the interactive survey on her Web site and voice mail system, Lillian has developed an e-mail list of more than 4,000 potential clients. She has also created an e-mail list of more than 350 law firms who might provide her with referrals. Each month, she writes a short newsletter on litigation and, in the blink of an eye, e-mails it to all these people.

By communicating daily through e-mail, newsgroups, and her World Wide Web chat room, Lillian is constantly meeting new potential clients on the Internet. Every day, her e-mail box has 20 to 30 messages from people wondering if they have grounds to sue someone. She assesses their situation and responds to each enquiry quickly. For those people she doesn't want to represent, she sends a standard rejection. For people she thinks have a case, she sends a detailed electronic form for them to fill out and return to her. Each day, she receives about ten electronic forms which she can review further. Using this process, she selects people she thinks will make the best kind of clients for her practice.

By using digital technology for marketing, Lillian has been able to attract a lot of new clients without extensive advertising. She does run a small ad in the Yellow Pages and the Saturday paper, but the ads promote the information she has available on the Internet and through the telephone and fax. Unlike her competitors who run expensive television ads, Lillian is able to save thousands of dollars using digital marketing techniques.

THE STRATEGIC DIGITAL BARTENDER

Bernie's Bar & Grill: Bernie the bartender runs one of the most popular pubs in the city. His customers frequent his establishment regularly. Everyone is amazed how he can remember everyone's name and favorite libation. None of them suspect that Bernie is actually a strategic digital bartender.

Bernie has created a very simple customer database tied into an equally simple promotional idea. Every time a new customer comes into his bar, Bernie offers him a free drink if he will pose for a picture. Using his digital camera, Bernie snaps the picture and downloads it immediately into his barside computer database. Bernie thanks him and asks him what he usually has to drink. He also invites the customer to enter a contest if he is willing to supply him with his address, telephone, and e-mail information. Using this simple method, Bernie has compiled a detailed database on more than 1,500 customers.

If someone comes into the bar and he can't recall his name, Bernie simply enters the person's general appearance (male, blond hair, short, beard; female, red hair, green eyes, athletic) into the search engine and the database presents the possible candidates. Within a few seconds, he can match up the face with the digital photo and then ask the customer if she would like to have her regular, "a dry martini." The customers at Bernie's Bar & Grill love the special treatment they receive. Unlike their experience at other restaurants and retail stores, the customers feel they're special when they come to Bernie's.

With this program in place, Bernie has taken his digital marketing program one giant step further. Bernie has placed his bar on the World Wide Web by setting up digital video cameras throughout his establishment. If a customer is sitting at home and thinking about going out, she can access Bernie's Web site and cruise through the bar to see what's happening. If she wants, she can make a reservation or order a drink in advance. (Bernie gives a 25 percent discount on all drinks ordered and paid for in advance over the Internet.) As well, cybersurfers can chat with other home-bound patrons in Bernie's private chatrooms. Many of the chatterers begin their conversation online and then meet at Bernie's later on in the evening.

In addition to his digital photo database and Web site, Bernie has introduced a smart card program for his best customers. Every time the customer spends money, Bernie slides the card into the processing slot attached to his computer. Credit points are automatically added to the card for future purchases, or a discount is given on the purchase by subtracting credit from the card. The customers love using the card because it actually contains the credit points. It feels like money in their pocket. As well, they can lend the card to friends and business associates as a gift. As long as someone knows the password, they can use the card.

Ongoing communication is the fourth component of Bernie's digital marketing strategy. Using the data in his customer database, Bernie distributes more than 1,500 newsletters every two months by fax and e-mail. The newsletters are individually addressed to each person, along with a report on the number of credit points they have on their smart card. The newsletter also contains special offers custom-tailored to the person's preferences. For example, if a customer has been ordering only vegetarian meals, Bernie sends her a coupon for a vegetarian dinner. If a customer likes to drink exotic imported beers, Bernie sends him a list of the new imports he has on tap.

All of these programs have helped Bernie keep customers coming back again and again. His marketing costs are relatively low compared to the money he used to spend on advertising in local newspapers and entertainment magazines.

REQUIEM FOR TRADITIONAL MARKETING

The marketing programs presented in this chapter signal the ascendancy of digital marketing and the subordination of traditional, mass-media promotional strategies. By combining digital technology with creative promotional ideas, you no longer need to rely on third-party intermediaries — such as wholesalers, retailers, and mass advertising media — to reach your customers and prospects. You can communicate directly with your customers using digital technology and digital promotional strategies. It just takes a little imagination and an understanding of how digital technology works.

In the next chapter, I will explain the last step in planning your digital marketing strategy — building your digital command center.

CHAPTER 11

BUILD YOUR DIGITAL COMMAND CENTER

Make it so.

Captain Jean-Luc Picard in
Star Trek: The Next Generation

The popularity of *Star Trek* is based, in part, upon our fascination with advanced technology. We're excited when Captain Picard orders his crew to take the starship *Enterprise* to another galaxy with the simple command "Make it so." In the distant future, it seems, we'll be able to entertain our merest whim by pushing a button or by telling a computer what we want done. Powerful machines will do the rest.

To succeed at digital marketing, you need to build your own version of the *Enterprise*. You need to develop a digital command center in your company to communicate on a day-by-day basis with your customers and prospects. Unlike a traditional marketing department — often far removed from direct contact with customers — a digital marketing department must be hardwired to customers. E-mail messages, for example, must be read and replied to within hours, if not minutes, and your Web site content may need to be updated and changed daily. In addition, your customer database should be constantly churning with new information uploaded from your salespeople, your customer service representatives, and your customers. To help you achieve these goals, this chapter explains what you need to do to organize your own digital command center.

INTEGRATION IN THE DIGITAL ECONOMY

To gather, store, process, and distribute digital information, you need to integrate your company into the digital economy. In the next three to five years, you will need the following capabilities in your company.

- Every computer is connected over a network using high-speed cable. This network includes an internal e-mail system that allows for the sending and receiving of Internet e-mail messages.
- Everyone involved in your company — employees, customers, and suppliers — are able to communicate by e-mail with everyone else in your company. As bandwidth becomes greater, you can upgrade your e-mail capability to include video-mail and live video-conferencing.
- Employees and contract workers are able to work at home, or at satellite offices, as easily as if they were in the office. Note: In the digital world, you may not have an office; your entire operation may run over a central server that electronically connects your organization.
- Your internal computer network is connected directly to the Internet over high-speed telephone or cable lines. This means every computer on your network is connected to the Internet at all times. In fact, it means your computer network is actually part of the Internet.
- You have security measures in place which restrict access to private corporate information on your network. One solution is to set up an Internet fire wall.

- Your marketing presentations, internal communications, and training courses exist in a multimedia format which combines text, graphics, sound, and video. You have software that allows for the easy development of multimedia content.
- You have one or many different types of online servers running on your network. This includes one or more Web servers, a BBS network server, and online database servers. Each of these servers are available to selected people within your organization over an Intranet, or outside your organization by way of the Internet.
- As an alternative to internal online servers, you can lease space with service bureaus. For example, you can rent space on a Web site that is halfway around the world. You can update its content as if the server was in your office. You may use a service bureau to set up and run your online BBS system. Remember, you don't need to buy expensive digital equipment in order to use it — you can rent it as well. Service bureaus exist for almost every digital tool mentioned in this book.
- Your customers access information about your business using a variety of digital communications tools including the telephone, fax, e-mail, the World Wide Web, interactive kiosks, and CD-ROM, and perhaps also through some sort of virtual reality (VR) device. Ideally, your customers are able to purchase your products and services electronically.
- You have an extensive database on all your customers and prospects. This database is relational in structure. (See Chapter 7.) All your digital communications and your digital marketing promotions are aimed at increasing the size, quality, and complexity of this database.
- All your computer systems are compatible. In the computer industry, this is known as "Open Systems Architecture." This means all your corporate information is accessible, no matter what type of computer is used. Also, your information should be accessible through all digital devices, not just computer-related ones.

- Your employees are fully fluent in the ways of basic digital technology. Everyone in your organization knows how to use the three major types of software programs: word processing, spreadsheet, and database. They are comfortable creating and viewing multimedia content. They understand the basic concepts of the Internet, and can find the information they need on it.

In order to succeed at digital marketing over the long term, you need to set up this type of infrastructure within your company. However, man didn't get to the moon in one day. So take it one step at a time. Here's an explanation of how to take the first steps:

GET ONLINE!

Your first step in digital marketing is to get online. You need to have a computer with access to the Internet including the World Wide Web, newsgroups, e-mail, FTP (File Transfer Protocol), and the host of other Internet platforms. If your company does not have a network-wide Internet connection, you need to subscribe to an Internet Service Provider (ISP) for an individual dial-up account. Of course, you will also need a modem attached to your computer.

A quality Internet dial-up account costs about $300 a year. There are many Internet providers on the market and pricing has become very competitive. However, a low-cost ISP may not have the capacity to provide quality service. With a bargain-basement ISP you may experience busy signals and slow access rates. And they may go out of business. So choose a high-quality supplier and pay the extra price. It's worth it in the long run.

When you get an Internet account, you receive an e-mail address. If you do not have a domain name registered (see Chapter 4), your address includes the domain name of your ISP such as bill_bishop@inforamp.net. If you have a domain name, you can use it for the second part of your e-mail address (i.e., bill_bishop@biginc.on.ca). If you want to register a domain name, your ISP can take care of it for you.

In addition, you receive a selection of software you can use to access the various platforms on the Internet. You receive a dialing program such as Winsock, which connects your computer to the Internet, along with applications such as a World Wide Web browser, Eudora to send and receive e-mail, and Fetch to conduct FTP.

Once you're online, you should spend time surfing the World Wide Web looking for ideas. Go to the search engines on the Web and look up your competitors. What are they doing on the Internet? Note any sites you find interesting. Notice the difference between sites which are merely advertising and those sites which attract people again and again.

SETTING UP A WEB SITE

After using the Internet for a while, you may wish to set up your own Web site. You can hire an outside consultant to help you, or learn how to do it yourself. In general, it's quite simple to set up a basic Home Page. You write the text in a word processing document and add codes called HTML tags. (HTML stands for Hyper Text Markup Language.) These tags, which you add to the text, indicate the font size and style, what graphics you want to display, and what other Web sites you want to link to. (There are many good books which explain the basics of the HTML language, or you can get HTML editors as shareware or as low-cost commercial software.) When you have your HTML document ready, you use FTP to send the file (along with the graphics files) to your ISP's Web server.

If you have a domain name, the address of your Web site can include it (such as www.biginc.on.ca). If you don't use (or have) your own domain name, your Web site address will include the domain of your ISP (such as www.inforamp.net/acme/). In most cases, use your domain name in your Web address because it's easier to remember and more professional. However, some ISPs charge more for Web sites if you use your domain name, so you may not want to incur the added cost.

Once the Web site is set up, there are two ongoing costs. Most Internet providers charge a monthly storage fee based on the number of bytes your files occupy on their server, and they may charge a data transfer fee for the number of bytes which are downloaded from your site. Negotiate carefully the data transfer fees with your ISP before launching your Home Page because you may end up paying a lot more than you bargained for if your site becomes really popular.

If you want to create something more than a basic Web site — with online surveys and multimedia functionality — you should get a professional consultant to create the site for you.

A NETWORK-WIDE INTERNET CONNECTION

To run a Web site from your office, you need to have a direct link from your network to the Internet. Without going into technical details, here is how it works. Your company's computers are joined to the Internet through a high-speed data line connected 24 hours a day to your Internet provider. A piece of hardware called a "router" directs the traffic coming and going between you and the Internet. This is called a network-wide Internet connection; it allows each of the computers in your office to access the Internet at all times, and allows you to set up a Web site on your network so people on the Internet can access it. It also means you can set up as many e-mail addresses as needed. For instance you can have bobs@biginc.on.ca, marym@bignc.on.ca, info@biginc.on.ca, customerservice@biginc.on.ca, and so on.

The cost of running a network-wide connection ranges from $500 to $1,000 per month. The price depends on the speed of your data lines and the amount of traffic on the network. You will need to purchase or lease the router (between $1,500 and $3,000), along with the Web server software.

INSTALL A BULLETIN BOARD SYSTEM (BBS)

In addition to a Web site, consider installing a BBS to electronically link your customers, associates, and suppliers. It will also serve as your internal e-mail system and allow you to access your computer network from home or on the road.

To set up a BBS you need a PC, server software, and modems. There are a number of good BBS software platforms on the market such as FirstClass™ and LotusNotes. You can set it up yourself or you can hire a consultant to install it.

With your BBS in place, you can give online accounts to your customers by supplying them with installation software. They will log into your system to send you e-mail, transfer computer files, and get information about your company. You can also create customized online order forms and searchable databases.

The cost of setting up a BBS ranges from $1,000 to $30,000 depending on the functions you need and the number of users you have. For example, if you have 100 users, you only need one or two modems. If you have 1,000 users, you need four or more modems. In addition, you may elect to place your BBS on the Internet. This allows users to access your system through their dial-up Internet accounts. This is useful if you have a lot of out-of-town users who use long distance to reach you. All these additional features cost money, but the important point is that even a small business can afford to run a BBS.

As discussed in Chapter 8, you can also hire a service bureau to run your BBS. Instead of setting up the hardware in your office, you connect by modem to the computers at the service bureau. The BBS runs in exactly the same way as an in-house system, except it costs a lot less to operate. As well, you don't need to worry about maintaining the software and the hardware. The only drawback is that you can't use the service bureau BBS to run your internal e-mail system.

OTHER DIGITAL CAPABILITIES

All the other digital capabilities you may need can be set up in-house or acquired through a service bureau. In general, which way you go depends on your needs and budget. I recommend, however, that you use a service bureau for your digital capabilities whenever possible because the service bureau incurs the cost of the hardware, and takes responsibility for maintaining and upgrading the equipment. These are important points because the technology is advancing rapidly. Many companies can't afford to keep upgrading their equipment every year. So let a service bureau do it instead.

Voice mail systems: If you want a basic voice mail system, you can run it through your telephone company. Bell Canada, for example, has the Call Answer service. If you're on the line, the service will pick up your call. This is ideal for a home office, but doesn't allow you to set up a menu of choices. If you want a more sophisticated system, you can set one up in your office, or hire a service bureau to intercept your calls. You can change the content on a service bureau's system just as easily as you can on an in-house system.

Fax-on-demand: You can set up a fax-on-demand system in your office with a PC and some easy-to-use software, or you can hire a service bureau to do it. Your job is to upload the content into the system and provide your audience with a directory of the available documents. Your customers and prospects don't care if they access your office or an outside service — they just want the information.

Long-distance calling cards: You need to use an outside supplier to run your calling card system because the switching equipment which processes the calls is connected to the telephone system. Your job is to design the card and develop content for the voice messages. It costs about $20,000 and up to run a calling card promotion. You pay for creative and technical development and for the printing of the cards. You also pay for the long-distance calls incurred by the recipients of your cards. This may be a fixed rate or based on the number of calls actually made with the cards.

Loyalty cards: If you're a retailer, consider setting up the equipment needed to process loyalty cards at your stores. You can install card readers which interface with your cash registers, or you can use card readers connected by modem to your central database. Some credit card companies now offer a loyalty card processing service to retailers. You distribute your loyalty cards to customers and process them using your credit card authorization system. The credit card company maintains the database for you. If you don't want to get fancy, you can process the cards manually. When a customer comes into your store with a loyalty card, you can enter the information directly into your database. Once again, you don't need to be a big company to run a loyalty program.

CONNECTING TO YOUR DATABASE

Wherever possible you need to connect your digital tools to your customer database. Ideally, the data entered by the customer — on your Web site survey form, or through your interactive voice-response system — is uploaded directly into your database. However, if you use a service bureau, this kind of direct link may not always be possible or affordable. In these cases, ask the service bureau to provide you with a file which you can import into your customer database. The point here is that you don't need to have a direct link to your database in order to gather customer data using digital tools.

A FUTURE MIGRATION PATH

This chapter has touched briefly on how to set up your digital command center. Obviously the technical details of installing digital equipment would fill dozens of books. Luckily there are many consultants who can help you actually install the equipment you need.

When deciding on which equipment to purchase or lease, look at your future migration path. Don't link up with any technology that doesn't give you the ability to upgrade or integrate it with other parts of your system. For example, you don't want to install a BBS which can't be connected to the Internet. You don't want to buy an interactive voice-response system which can't be linked to your database. So before you start buying equipment and setting up peripherals, sketch out a plan for your entire system. Put together a diagram which shows the links between each digital tool and your customer database. Don't look at each tool as a separate thing. Look at each tool as a component of an overall digital marketing system.

READY TO ROCK 'N' ROLL

If you have been following step-by-step the chapters in this section, you have:

- created your Digital Vision — you know what business objectives you want to achieve over the long, medium, and short terms;
- researched your market to determine the digital capabilities of your customers and prospects;
- set up your customer database;
- chosen the digital tools most appropriate for your customers and prospects;
- chosen your digital promotion idea which will attract people to your Digital Domain;
- put together your digital tools, customer database, and promotional ideas into a complete digital marketing program; and
- built your digital command center.

Now is the moment you've been waiting for — the launch of your digital marketing program.

SECTION THREE

RUNNING YOUR DIGITAL MARKETING PROGRAM

CHAPTER 12

LAUNCH YOUR DIGITAL MARKETING PROGRAM

We have lift off.

Neil Armstrong to Mission Control
Apollo 11, 1969

Your digital marketing program is like the Saturn V rocket that launched Neil Armstrong and his crew to the moon. The tremendous power needed to launch the rocket consumed most of its fuel in the first few minutes. But once the spacecraft was on its way, only minor adjustments were needed. So it is with your digital marketing program. It's like a rocket — it has three distinct stages and needs you to send it skyward with a blast. The stages are:

- the Launch;
- the Ongoing Process; and
- the Expansion of your Program.

Let's take a look at each of these stages.

THE LAUNCH

When you're ready for liftoff, you can generate initial awareness of your promotion using both digital and mass-media marketing tools. The appropriate mix of these tools depends on the technical capabilities of your audience and the type of promotion you're launching.

Mass-media promotions:

- **Advertising**: Advertising in the mass media can be an important vehicle for generating initial awareness of your digital promotion. Because it's intrusive, advertising in newspapers, magazines, on television, and on billboards will make people aware of your digital promotion. You can advertise the address of your Web site on the side of a bus, or use an airplane to skywrite your domain name. You can place the telephone number for your Cellular Comedy Club on a highway billboard, or run an ad in a trade magazine announcing the launch of your new CD-ROM.
- **Publicity**: In addition to advertising, you can send out a news release to the media announcing the launch of your digital promotion. In the release, stress the value of the information you have to offer or emphasize the unique and useful nature of your digital service. Provide the media with pictures and graphic representations of your promotion. For example, if you're launching a Web site, send the media a picture of your Home Page. If you're launching a long-distance calling card, send them a picture of it. (Don't just send them the card — they might not think to take a picture of it.)
- **Direct mail**: Direct mail is another useful way to promote the launch of your digital promotion. For example, if you send out a monthly billing, include a flyer in the envelope about your loyalty card program. If you publish a newsletter, write an article on the front page about your new BBS. If you have a customer database, print out the list and send your customers an announcement about your new fax-on-demand service.

- **Packaging and point-of-sale**: You can advertise your digital promotion on packaging and point-of-sale material. If you run a brewery, put your Web site address on the label of your beer bottles. If you make toothpaste, put your e-mail address on the tube. If you sell potato chips, run a digital contest and put your calling card number on point-of-sale counter displays. Of course, don't forget to put the location of your digital promotions on your stationery and fax cover pages.

Digital promotions: If your promotion is aimed at online users, there are a number of ways to launch it using digital and online technology. Unlike traditional mass-media advertising, most of these digital promotions can be done for free or little cost.

- **Search engines**: If you create a Web site, you should list it on the major search engines such as Yahoo and Excite. Each search engine has an electronic form for you to indicate the address of your site along with a description of its contents. When someone using the search engine enters your company name, or a key word describing your products or services, your company's site is included somewhere in the listing. Basic listings on most search engines are free. Tip: When writing the description of your site, use single descriptive words only. If the site describes a yachting company, use words such as boats, yachting, sailing, cruising, bareboating, chartering. That way, you maximize the number of possible words which will call up your Web site on the search engine.
- **Web site display advertising**: You can place an interactive display ad on one of the popular Web sites. For example, you can place an advertisement on the Yahoo search engine. When people access Yahoo, they see your ad. If they want to see your site, they simply click on the ad. The cost of running a Web ad can range from a few hundred dollars to hundreds of thousands. It all depends on the amount of traffic generated by the host site. As I've contended a few times in this book, I believe this kind of online advertising should be billed based solely on results. In this case, you should only pay for the number of

visits you receive from the host site. If you don't get any visits, you pay nothing; if you get thousands of visits, you pay more. If you can, negotiate this kind of results-only program.

- **Web site links and pointers**: To generate traffic on your Web site, you want people to discover your existence on other sites. For example, if you have a site about fishing supplies, you want to be listed on all major sites frequented by anglers. You can approach the owners of the sites and ask them to display a hypertext listing of your site. If it's a really popular site, they may ask you to pay them, or you may be able to negotiate a reciprocal deal by which you list them if they list you. Take a look around the World Wide Web and find the sites which would be visited by your target audience. Then send them an e-mail message asking them to point people to your site.
- **Newsgroups**: If you have an interesting story to tell, you may be able to promote your Web site in a newsgroup. If you're launching a site about knitting, for example, you can send a message to a knitting newsgroup describing the useful information found on your site. But keep this in mind: newsgroups are not intended for commercial purposes; they're for people to discuss particular subjects. So be careful using newsgroups for promotion. You don't want to aggravate the people in a newsgroup by being too commercial in your approach. Tip: If you want to use newsgroups to develop business relationships, spend a lot of time participating in one or two key groups. Offer useful advice to the members. Think of it as public relations rather than advertising.
- **E-mail**: Be careful about using e-mail to launch your promotion. Don't send out hundreds of unsolicited e-mail messages announcing your program. You'll get back a lot of nasty e-mail messages. You can even be kicked off the Internet by your service provider. However, you can use e-mail to send out messages to your existing customers if they have given you prior permission. That's why it's important to put e-mail addresses in your customer database, even if you aren't ready to launch a digital promotion. Once you are, you can use these addresses

to send out an announcement. Once again, I reiterate: Don't send out unsolicited e-mail messages. Get permission first.

- **Internet mailing lists**: If there is an Internet mailing list related to your business, you can subscribe to the list and promote your Web site on it. For example, if you have a Web site about personal finance, you can subscribe to a mailing list about retirement planning. As a subscriber, you can send a message to the list server which will automatically distribute it to everyone who subscribes to the list. As with newsgroups and e-mail, you have to be careful with this strategy. If you appear to be too self-serving, you will raise the ire of the other members and possibly find yourself expelled from the list. Once again, think public relations, not advertising.
- **Commercial online services**: You can promote the launch of your digital promotion on one or more of the commercial online services such as CompuServe, Prodigy, America Online, and the Microsoft Network. If you have a specific target audience, these services may have special conferences that cater to them. For example, a tennis racquet manufacturer may want to participate in a tennis-related conference on America Online. Commercial network online advertising is expensive compared to other online promotions, but it may be able to deliver to your target audience.
- **Public BBS networks**: In spite of the growing popularity of the Internet and the World Wide Web, BBS networks are still going strong. There are thousands of BBSs across North America covering every imaginable topic. In most cases, they're free to join. Directories of BBSs are available at libraries and bookstores. If you find a BBS that caters to your target audience, you can log in and announce the launch of your digital promotion.

Promoting the launch of your BBS: When launching a BBS, you want to get a lot of people using it as quickly as possible. It's a chicken-and-egg scenario: to get a lot of people using your BBS, you need to have a lot of activity on the system; to generate a lot of activity, you need a lot of people using it. For this reason, you need to do something at the beginning to get the ball rolling.

For example, if you're setting up a BBS for an association, give the service away for free to the first 200 subscribers (if it's a fee-based service), or enlist a core group of people who will use it actively in the early stages. The initial group will generate a lot of messages, and this activity will attract additional subscribers. Once you reach a critical mass of users and activity, the system will take on a life of its own.

Direct mail and telemarketing are two traditional tools you can use to launch your BBS. You can mail out installation packages to your potential subscribers. The package should contain a disk (with the connection software), installation instructions, and promotional material on the benefits of the system. Also, you can call your potential subscribers and find out if they have a computer and a modem. If they do, you can send them an installation package.

You can also use the Internet and commercial online services to launch your BBS. For example, you can put the connection software for your BBS on a Web site. If someone is interested in joining the BBS, they download the software from your site and install it on their computer. This saves you the trouble and cost of mailing a disk to new subscribers.

In general, the proactive approach is the best way to get a BBS started. If you want people to connect electronically to your company, go to their home or office and set up the system on their computer. You need to be proactive because many people do not have the motivation or the inclination to install new capabilities on their computer. But once the software is set up, they will use the BBS to communicate with your company. So get out there and be proactive.

THE ONGOING PROCESS

Following the successful launch of your program, keep it exciting and vibrant by constantly changing the content, and look for new opportunities. Unlike traditional marketing, digital marketing is an ongoing interactive process.

The four-activities process: The digital marketing process is comprised of four ongoing activities: gathering, storing, processing, and distributing digital information. How efficiently and creatively you perform these activities determines the long-term success of your digital marketing program.

1. Gather information: Using digital tools such as smart cards, interactive voice mail, online survey forms, and point-of-sale equipment, you gather information about your customers and place it in a database. You also gather content for your digital promotions such as text, graphics, pictures, sound, and video.

2. Store digital information: You store digital information and make it available to your employees, suppliers, and customers. For example, you can provide your customers with an online database of bonsai tree farms, or place digital audio messages on your interactive voice mail system.

3. Process information: You assemble your digital information into different forms. For example, you can pull together text, sound, and graphics to create a Web site, or process data in your customer database to generate a report on spending patterns.

4. Distribute information: You distribute information using a variety of digital and traditional tools. For example, you can send out weekly e-mail messages to all your customers on the Internet.

When your digital marketing program is under way, you do all four of these activities on a day-to-day basis. You must deal with the constant flow of digital information. You store some of the bits and discard the rest. You take the stored data and process it into many different forms. And then you distribute the reassembled bits to your customers and prospects. Then you repeat the cycle.

To help you manage this process, here are a few words of advice:

- Delegate someone as the administrator of the digital marketing process. His or her job is to keep the flow of bits and bytes moving efficiently through the system.
- Use digital technology to automate the flow of bits and bytes whenever possible.
- Eliminate the manual entry of customer data by gathering it using digital tools, such as online survey forms and interactive voice mail.
- Use automated software, such as fax and e-mail broadcast utilities, to distribute digital information. For example, you can use an e-mail list server to notify customers when you've made changes to your Web site or BBS.

So remember: digital marketing is an ongoing process. Unlike traditional marketing, you can't just run some advertising and wait for the telephone to ring. You have to be actively involved on a continuous basis.

THE EXPANSION OF YOUR PROGRAM

As time goes by, you'll want to expand your digital marketing program. You might start off with a Web site and then decide to produce a CD-ROM or add an interactive voice-response system. You might decide to add a calling card loyalty program or a fax-on-demand system. The key is to make sure any equipment you buy is compatible with your existing infrastructure. Ideally, you want all your digital tools and processes to be compatible.

The digital tool most important to expand is your customer database. As the amount of customer information grows, analyze and segment it regularly. Ask yourself: "Are there new markets I should pursue? Are there new segments I should target with special promotions? Are there new products and services I can offer these segments?"

If you're thinking about adding a new element to your digital marketing program, return to your original plan. Ask yourself: "Does this new component help me realize my Digital Vision? Does it fit into the digital profile of my customer database? Will it attract people to my Digital Domain?" If you ask yourself these questions, you'll know which expansion ideas make sense, and which ones don't. The important thing is to keep your digital marketing program on track by constantly referring to your original vision.

In the next chapter, I look at how to figure out if your digital marketing program is working.

CHAPTER 13

ASSESS YOUR DIGITAL SUCCESS

Of course some of their animals undoubtedly consisted of electronic circuitry fakes, too; he had of course never nosed into the matter, any more than they, his neighbors, had pried into the real workings of his sheep. Nothing could be more impolite. To say, "Is your sheep genuine?" would be a worse breach of manners than to inquire whether a citizen's teeth, hair, or internal organs would test out authentic.

Do Androids Dream of Electric Sheep?
Philip K. Dick, 1968

Since the invention of the printing press, marketers have been trying to assess the effectiveness of mass-media promotions. If you run a television or magazine ad, how do you know if it's working? If you put up a highway billboard, how do you know you're getting your money's worth? If you send out a direct mail piece, what response rate is sufficient?

To provide answers to these questions has become an industry in itself. There are hundreds of auditing bureaus which provide statistics on gross rating points (GRP), total impressions, total audience, share of audience, audited circulation, response rates, and so on. In general, these assessment tools must be viewed with a bit of skepticism. No matter how scientific these assessment methods sound, they almost always require a leap of faith. It's almost impossible to tell the difference between the real sheep and the electric sheep.

HITS, HITS, HITS

With the advent of digital marketing — especially the explosion of the World Wide Web, there has been a rush to develop a standard way to assess the impact of a Web site. In most cases, sites are assessed by the number of "hits" they receive. Web site operators proclaim their sites have millions of hits per month. People read about this and say "Wow! That means millions of people have looked at the site." But this is far from the truth. The emphasis on hits is totally erroneous, and if it continues, it will severely damage the credibility of the Web as a marketing tool.

Each hit on a Web site does *not* mean a new person has looked at the site. A hit is registered every time a text or graphics file is downloaded. If you have five graphic files on your Home Page, every time someone looks at it, six hits will be registered, five for the graphics and one for the text file. If a person looks through your whole site, hundreds of hits may be registered in a single visit! That's why the emphasis on hits is so ludicrous. As an assessment tool, it is almost meaningless.

Fortunately, there are many other ways to gauge the effectiveness of your Web site. Instead of counting hits, you can use automated Web tracking software to count the following:

- **Total visits**: This measures the number of times a person visits your site. If a particular person accesses your site five times, it counts as five visits.
- **Unique visits**: This is the number of times someone from a new domain name visits your site in a given reporting period. If your site is accessed from 500 different domain names in a month, you have had 500 unique visits. If someone from a

domain name accesses your site ten times in a month, you have had one unique visit. (This method of assessing the popularity of a Web site is misleading because you don't know how many different individuals accessed your site.)

- **Total anonymous enquiries**: If you run a survey on your site that does not require the participants to leave their names, you can track the number of anonymous enquiries.
- **Total online forms completed**: I believe this is the most credible tool for measuring the usefulness of your site, and your digital promotion in general. Count the number of times someone fills out a survey form, and gives you his name and e-mail address. One person giving you this information is worth 50,000 anonymous hits because you have started your one-to-one relationship with him. Remember, the point of digital marketing is to develop relationships — not to generate reports on domain names and file downloads.
- **Total sales generated**: Ultimately, you want to know how many sales you generated because of your Web site. If you have an online store, it's easy to determine how many online sales you have made. If your sales happen offline, it's much harder to draw a connection between your Web site and a sale. However, there is a way. If you maintain a customer database, you can track how a person originally found out about your company. If the customer makes a purchase a year from now, you can look him up in the database and see if he has ever completed your online form. Or you can ask the customer how he heard about you. If he says, "On the World Wide Web," enter this into the database. At the end of each month, you can compile a report on all the sales generated by people who learned about your company on the Internet or through other digital tools. Then you will know if the money invested in a particular digital tool is justified by the sales it generates.

INVALID ASSESSMENT TOOLS

If someone tries to sell you a promotional opportunity on the Internet, or on another digital medium, watch out for these buzz words:

- **Length of stay**: This measures the length of time that someone spends at your site. However, it doesn't tell you if she was actually looking at it or listening to it. For example, if someone logs onto your Web site, and leaves it on her screen all day, does that visit count as a 24-hour stay? Obviously not, but it will increase the average length of stay and give you an inaccurate profile of the actual situation.
- **Number of bytes requested**: This measures the total number of bytes downloaded from a Web site in a given reporting period. This is not a particularly useful measuring tool. If a site has a lot of huge graphics files, it will register a lot of bytes even if the traffic is light.
- **Number of "eyes"**: It measures the number of people who have looked at a site in a reporting period. However, as explained, it is impossible to determine how many different people looked at your site, unless you require them to leave their names.

THE PROBLEM OF DISK CACHING

When you download a file from a Web site, it is usually stored on your hard drive using a process called "disk caching." It is used to speed up your surfing of the Internet. If you go back to a page you were previously viewing, it is reloaded from your hard drive, rather than from the original site. Because of disk caching, people may be seeing your site more often than you know about. As well, due to the heavy traffic congestion on the World Wide Web, Internet service providers are starting to store large disk caches of the most popular Web sites. In this way, people can access your site from an ISP disk cache, rather than from the original site. This means a lot of people might see your Home Page, but it won't register on your original Web site. Consequently, as people use, and become more aware of disk caching, hits will be rendered an unreliable and irrelevant assessment tool.

ASSESSING WEB DISPLAY ADVERTISING

If you run a display ad on a popular Web site, you can track the number of visits you receive from that ad. For example, if you place an ad on a page within the Yahoo search engine, you can track how many people come to your site by way of the ad. This is a valid way to assess the ad's impact, but it also brings into question the advertising fee structure. It's my contention that you should only pay for the number of unique visits you receive from an Internet ad. Unlike a magazine or TV advertisement, you should only pay if you get results.

MEASURING QUALITY AND CONTACT

Instead of counting hits and unique visits, measure the quality of the contact you make with your customers and prospects. Set up an interactive form for people to fill out. Make sure your database contains their names and other useful information. Assess the impact of your Web site, or any other digital marketing tool, based on the number of new prospects you meet, and the number of existing customers who use it. Because digital technology is so functionally interactive, you don't need to be satisfied with counting hits and other mass-media-type assessment models. You can insist on specific measurements of actual sales generated by a digital tool.

MEASURING OTHER DIGITAL TOOLS

BBS: There are a number of ways to assess the impact of a private BBS network. You can measure the number of users you attract, the amount of time used on the system, and the use of online forms. While all these quantitative measurements are valid, it is probably better to assess the qualitative impact of your network. Ask your clients how they like using it. Do they like the features on it? Would they like to see additional functions built in to the system? You can place electronic surveys on the network or survey people in person or over the telephone. If they use the system regularly and express satisfaction with it, you know your BBS is working well.

Loyalty card programs: You can measure the success of a loyalty card program based on the number of members, the amount of points they accumulate, and by the increased sales generated by the program. You can also measure its success by analyzing how much you're learning about your customers. Is the program helping you to better understand what your customers want and need? Is it helping you develop a better relationship with them? If so, your loyalty program is doing its job.

Calling card promotions: When you distribute a promotional long-distance calling card, you can count the number of people who use the card, the amount of long-distance time they consume, the number of interactive voice advertisements they listen to. Once again, the best measurement is based on the number of people who complete the interactive voice survey.

DATABASE TRACKING

I believe all this emphasis on "hits" and "unique visits" is irrelevant. If you develop a strategic digital marketing program, you don't need to bother with this nonsense. Your objective is to increase profits by starting and fostering more business relationships. If a digital tool generates increased profits, it's working; if it helps you start or improve a relationship, it's working. If it doesn't, at least, attract people who are willing to leave their name with you, it isn't working.

Using your customer database is the only meaningful way to determine if a digital tool is helping you develop worthwhile relationships. It works something like this. Every person who leaves his or her name — on a Web site, interactive kiosk, BBS, calling card system, or smart card terminal — should be entered into your customer database. Which tool the person used should be recorded along with the name. When the person makes a purchase, you can track it back to his or her first encounter with you. If over time you find that a digital tool isn't generating any sales, drop it or change your approach.

In the next section, I look at the ethics of digital marketing, specifically the issues of personal privacy, data security, copyright, and trademark protection.

SECTION FOUR

THE ETHICS OF DIGITAL MARKETING

CHAPTER 14

PROTECTING CUSTOMER PRIVACY

The telescreen received and transmitted simultaneously. Any sound that Smith made, above the level of a very low whisper, would be picked up by it. You had to live — did live, from the habit that became instinct — in the assumption that every sound you made was overheard, and, except in darkness, every movement scrutinized.

Nineteen Eighty-Four
George Orwell, 1949

Is Big Brother watching your every move? Is he entering the information in a database? As digital and online technology becomes more pervasive in our society, people are asking these questions. And for good reason. Somewhere, a database knows where you shop, what you buy, what you eat, who you call, where you travel, and who you are likely to vote for in the next election. Every time you use your credit card or telephone, it is recorded in a database. Every time you send an e-mail message or make a cellular telephone call, someone could be eavesdropping. Taken to an extreme level, this type of digital surveillance is frightening to both consumers and marketers.

That's why the issue of personal privacy is an important subject to study. If you act responsibly, you can use information gathered by digital tools to foster better relationships with your customers. If you act irresponsibly, you can damage your business relationships and perhaps face criminal charges.

THE POTENTIAL FOR ABUSE

As more companies and organizations develop extensive customer databases, the potential for abuse grows. Make sure you don't engage in the four types of database abuse which infringe upon the personal privacy of your customers.

Unauthorized data sharing: Recently the Ontario Medical Association (OMA) complained to the Ontario College of Pharmacists about the sharing of database information between pharmacists and pharmaceutical companies. The pharmacists, who gather data on what drugs doctors prescribe, sold this information to a private company, which in turn, sold it to drug companies. In other words, the pharmacists were selling information about their customers (the doctors) without first getting their permission.

Although the pharmacists did not break any laws, they damaged their bond of trust with doctors. By trying to make a few extra dollars, they alienated many of their best customers and generated negative media publicity which tarnished their public image. The OMA did not take legal action, but recommended that database information be shared only under the following conditions:

- Patient confidentiality is maintained at all times.
- Written permission for full disclosure of the data is obtained from the physician prior to the release by the pharmacists of personalized prescriber information.
- The companies collecting this information agree to send cumulative data back to the physicians for educational purposes.

The lesson to be learned from this situation is clear. The pharmacists could have saved themselves a lot of grief if they had simply asked the doctors for permission to sell the data. If the answer had been no, they wouldn't have done it. If the answer had been yes, they would have been free to share the data with the drug companies, and to profit from their efforts in an ethical manner.

Data integration: Another potential abusive practise is the unauthorized integration of databases by two or more companies or organizations. If two companies integrate their databases, they can develop an extremely detailed profile of an individual. While this sounds appealing, the practise is unethical because the customer has no idea that information about him or her is being shared between two companies.

Unethical data utilization: If a company uses data for a purpose not originally intended, they are breaking the contract of trust with their customers. For example, a telephone company can figure out if you call a lot of 1-800 numbers to order products. It can also figure out what products you are calling to order. It could sell this information to a company that wants to target people who use 1-800 numbers to buy certain kinds of products. A credit card company, for example, could figure out what kind of restaurants you like to patronize, and sell that information to a cook book publisher who could send you unsolicited and unwanted junk mail.

Unauthorized public disclosure: If you disclose to the public information about a customer without her permission, you are acting unethically. For example, a video store could provide the media with a list of videos rented by a prominent politician. If the list contained pornography, the disclosure of this information could force the politician's resignation.

Although all these practises are not illegal, avoiding them is in your own best interest. You could be sued by a customer or a group of customers, but the most important reason to act ethically is to maintain the trust of your customers. If people suspect you use information about them in an unethical way, they will not provide you with any more information. They probably won't be buying your goods and services either.

SAFEGUARD THE BOND OF TRUST

One major goal of digital marketing is to establish better relationships with your customers. Like all relationships, this relationship is based on trust. If you earn the trust of your customer, your relationship will strengthen; if you violate this trust, your relationship will deteriorate or end altogether.

Trust is earned by communicating openly and honestly with your customers and prospects. If you ask someone to fill in an interactive survey, tell him what you are going to use it for. If you plan to share the information, tell him with whom and in what manner, and ask for permission. If a customer wants to be removed from your database, do so immediately. As well, give him access to the information you have about him.

To maintain the trust of your customers, you also need to safeguard the information you have about them. You need to establish security measures to keep your database out of the hands of competitors and dishonest employees.

Digital marketing code of ethics: Although no formal code of ethics exists for digital marketing, many organizations have developed privacy guidelines which can be applied to the digital marketplace. The Canadian Direct Marketing Association (CDMA) has a code of ethics based, in part, upon privacy guidelines issued by the Organization of Economic Cooperation & Development (OECD). In general, these guidelines state:

- Gather and store only information which is pertinent to your business. For example, a retail chain should not compile medical records and police reports related to their customers.
- Collect data directly from your customers, not from other companies or organizations.
- Tell your customers how you plan to use the data.
- Only use the data for the originally intended purpose. If you wish to use it for another purpose, get permission from each customer involved.
- If requested, let your customers see what information you have about them.
- Remove customers from your database if they ask you to do so.
- Take appropriate security measures to ensure your customer data does not fall into other hands.

Other digital tools: In addition to using databases in an ethical manner, you need to use the other digital tools in a manner which protects the privacy of your customers:

- Do not read your customer's private e-mail messages on your private BBS network unless you receive prior permission, or you are compelled to audit them due to a suspicion of criminal activity (see next chapter).
- Do not monitor the viewing patterns of individual customers on your Web site pages or BBS unless you have their prior permission.
- Do not intercept data or analyze digital information transmitted by customers on your industry-wide information system.

Privacy ombudsman: Consider appointing a privacy ombudsman to champion your customers' right to privacy. The privacy ombudsman should have the authority to review all activities related to your customer database, and to cancel any activities that contravene the digital marketing code of ethics.

Government regulations: Only a few jurisdictions have developed laws or guidelines pertaining to digital marketing. On the federal level, Industry Canada has penned a report called Privacy and the Information Highway. In January 1994, Quebec passed the first privacy legislation introduced in North America. As the public becomes more concerned about their privacy, politicians will be called upon to develop laws governing digital marketing.

Self-regulation: Even if laws are passed restricting what you can do with digital information, it will still be in your best interest to regulate yourself. As discussed, your customers will not tolerate any breach of their personal privacy. Even if you don't break any laws, you could lose your customers by using your database in an unethical manner.

OPEN COMMUNICATION — KEY TO ETHICAL DIGITAL MARKETING

If you engage in open, two-way communication with you customers and prospects, you will avoid most of the ethical problems associated with digital marketing. Explain the benefits of your database to your customers. Explain how you will and won't use the data. Give them the complete story. If you want to use the data for something, ask your customers for permission.

If you communicate openly, you won't need to be defensive about your customer database. From the customers' perspective, your database is also a useful tool to save them time and money. When they call you, you can access information about them in seconds. If they have a question about a product, you can look up their order in a matter of seconds. If they have a problem, you can quickly verify warranty information. And you never have to ask them twice for the correct spelling of their name.

In the final analysis, digital marketing should be viewed as a collaborative enterprise between you and your customers. You gather information from your customers to serve them better. They provide you with the information because they trust you will use the data in an ethical manner, and won't share it with other people without their permission.

A Final Word on Data Sharing: If you are determined to share your data, a common practise is to sell your mailing list containing only names and addresses. You may feel this is acceptable because it leaves out the other data you've collected. However, you should first ask yourself if this practise fits into the kind of relationship you want to have with your customers.

OWNERSHIP OF PERSONAL DATA

As information about each individual becomes more valuable, it may come to pass that each person is given ownership of his or her data with all the legal protection of copyright. For example, if a marketer wishes to share information about you, she would have to seek your permission, and give you a royalty on the money earned. Although this type of system may be unenforceable at present, the future emergence of "privacy agents" and "digital privacy intermediaries" may make it a reality.

Privacy agents: A privacy agent is someone who acts on behalf of individuals to ensure they are financially compensated for the use and exchange of their personal data. For example, if someone wants information about you, they approach the agent and negotiate a price. If the marketer wants more information, the agent gathers it from you and sells it to the marketer. Although the marketer can try to get the information directly from you, it is much easier and ultimately less expensive for her to get it through your privacy agent. Of course, you always have the right to refuse a request for information.

The profession of privacy agent could become big business in the digital age. A privacy agency will sign you up and build a huge database dossier on your lifestyle, buying habits, preferences, needs, and wants. You will receive a sign-up commission, plus a royalty on all contracts signed with marketers. Marketers will pay privacy agents to reach new prospects because the data they provide is timely, accurate, and comprehensive.

Digital privacy intermediaries: As the amount of marketing information explodes in the digital economy, services will spring up to help you keep your personal privacy, while helping you get the information you need. I call these services Digital Privacy Intermediaries (DPI). For example, a DPI provides each client with a private fax mailbox. As a subscriber, you fill out a monthly survey indicating what products and services you're interested in buying over the next few months. Your DPI reviews promotional material from marketers (who pay to use the service) and sends information which matches your stated needs to your fax mailbox. The marketers do not know your identity, yet they know they're reaching you with information you have requested As a subscriber, the benefits are substantial: You receive a free fax mailbox, get the information you want, and protect your privacy all at the same time. Digital Privacy Intermediaries can also offer their services using voice mailboxes, BBSs, Web sites, and CD-ROMs.

As time goes on, DPIs will become a primary digital marketing tool for reaching new prospects. The cost of sending a promotional message through a DPI will be much higher than it is for mass direct mail, but a DPI system will provide a much more targeted audience. Of course, once the prospect responds to your message (distributed through the DPI), you can enter them into your customer database, if they consent.

Request for Proposal (RFP) robots: In addition to DPIs, people will use digital, Request For Proposal (RFP) robots to get information they need while protecting their privacy. Using a RFP robot, you post an anonymous e-mail message to indicate what products and services you are looking for. Digital marketers scan the RFP entries and pick out the ones which pertain to their business. They find out what you need and send you, by e-mail, promotional material about the products/services you requested. If you're interested in what they're selling, you can call or e-mail the company. In this way, you get the information you want while keeping your anonymity.

SENSITIVITY TO THE NEED FOR PRIVACY

As a digital marketer, you must be sensitive to your customers' need for privacy. Instead of trying to invade this privacy through intrusive telemarketing or by sharing your customer database, make it your commitment to protect their privacy. Make public your digital marketing code of ethics. Be honest and open about how you build and use your customer database. When planning a digital marketing program, put yourself in the shoes of your customer. Ask yourself: "Would I want someone to use information about me in this manner?" If the answer is "no," you'll know what to do.

In the next chapter, I look at how to protect your digital rights, including the issues of copyright, trademark infringement, and data security.

CHAPTER 15

PROTECTING YOUR DIGITAL RIGHTS

It was a pleasure to burn. It was a special pleasure to see things eaten, to see things blackened and changed. With the brass nozzle in his fists, with this great python spitting its venomous kerosene upon the world, the blood pounded in his head, and his hands were the hands of some amazing conductor playing all the symphonies of blazing and burning to bring down the tatters and charcoal ruins of history.

Fahrenheit 451
Ray Bradbury, 1950

Ray Bradbury's book *Fahrenheit 451* chronicles the attempt by a totalitarian government to control the flow of information by making it illegal to read and write books. To choke off the free exchange of ideas, "firemen" burn books whenever they are uncovered. ("Fahrenheit 451" refers to the temperature at which books burn.)

Instead of books, Bradbury could have written about digital and online technology. The free exchange of information across national boundaries over the Internet has bureaucrats and policing agencies around the world frantically searching for ways to control the flow of bits and bytes. Are we coming to the day when governments will "burn" digital and online communications? Will criminal activity on the Internet necessitate some type of online policing, or should cyberspace be left unfettered by any type of control? The questions are important and must be answered, but the reality is: regulatory matters — such as copyright and trademark protection — which have been traditionally legislated and enforced by governments, have become virtually unenforceable in the digital age. Even if they want to, governments cannot control or regulate the global flow of digital information. But it's not only governments which are worried about digital and online technology; marketers are concerned too. Take, for example, the Domain Name Dilemma.

DOMAIN NAME DILEMMA

The issue of digital trademark and copyright protection has become a hornet's nest since the commercialization of the World Wide Web. As discussed in Chapter 4, you need to register a domain name if you want to do business on the World Wide Web. Network Solutions, which handles the registration of domain names, has been doling them out on a first-come, first-serve basis, regardless of who owns the trademark. But now that companies are waking up to the commercial potential of the Web, they are screaming foul if the name they want has been taken by someone else, especially if they have a federal trademark protecting the name.

In a test case, Roadrunner Computer Systems sued Network Solutions. The computer company was upset because Warner Brothers was given the right to the domain name, roadrunner.com, even though the computer company had secured it months before with Network Solutions. The registrar sided with Warner Brothers because the television and movie company owns a US federal trademark on the word "Roadrunner." However, the computer company was not to be outdone. They acquired a federal trademark for "roadrunner" as well — but in Tunisia, not in the United States. Roadrunner Computer Systems had read the fine print of the domain name guidelines which stated that federally registered trademarks have priority. But it doesn't say from which federal government — the US, China, Tunisia, or any other country.

In another case, the Academy of Motion Picture Arts and Sciences lost a case it filed against Network Solutions regarding the use of the domain names "academyaward.com" and "oscar.com." Senior US District Court Judge Waters said Network Solutions did not infringe on the Academy's trademark by granting the domain names to another organization. Judge Waters ruled that "the mere registration of a domain name does not constitute commercial use, and does not prove irreparable injury resulted from the registration of the domain name by another party."

Hundreds of other similar cases are cropping up as companies start to use the Internet and digital technology for marketing. Because of the problems associated with copyright and trademark on the Internet, in the next few years thousands of companies will battle to wrestle control of domain names. Companies from different countries and different industries will claim the trademark rights for the same domain names. As a solution, Internet administrators are thinking about introducing new domain name levels in addition to .com, such as .biz, .sports, or .ent. However, I believe this will confuse the issue further. Companies will want to register all the possible domain names using their trademark — for example, acme.com, acme.biz, acme.ent. New domain name levels won't address the conflict between domain names and trademarks.

Because of this confusion in the Internet community, I advise you to register your domain name now. If you wait, you might miss out or face the prospect of a legal battle.

THE IMPOSSIBLE TASK OF DIGITAL ENFORCEMENT

Because it's so easy to capture, store, process, and redistribute digital information, it is becoming almost impossible to police trademark and copyright infractions on the Internet. Consider for example, the problem of the Digital Fan.

The digital fan: Let's say you own a major rollerblade hockey team, the Hanover Hippos. Your team has won the world championships three times in a row, and made you millions of dollars selling merchandise and information about the Hippos. You've created your official Hippo Home Page, and receive more than a million hits a week. But something is amiss. Many of your fans are starting to set up their own online fan clubs. They're plastering the Hippo logo all over their pages and posting statistics and player profiles downloaded from your site. In addition, fans of your archrivals, the Neustadt Nimrods, have set up anti-Hippo sites filled with lewd images which they have made by digitally altering your logo.

After a review of these sites, you realize you have to deal with more than 250 infractions of your copyright and trademarks. And more troublesome, half of the perpetrators are loyal fans — 20 percent of them are from Europe and Asia, and 65 percent of them are under the age of 14. Your lawyers tell you that you can take legal action, but it will cost millions and prove to be a public relations nightmare. You consider shutting down your Home Page, but you know it won't do any good. Digital versions of your logo have become so widespread on the Internet that you will never be able to curtail their use.

The finger in the digital dike: As the case of the Digital Fan illustrates, trying to control the use of copyright material on the Internet is like trying to keep out the sea with your finger in a dike. In the days of mass media, it was much easier to enforce trademarks and copyright, and much harder to violate them. In the past, if someone wanted to use your logo, they had to reproduce it in some way or broadcast it over television or radio. If they wanted to use your text copy, they had to print a newspaper, or publish a book. The physical reality of traditional media made it expensive and time-consuming to infringe on someone's rights. It also made it obvious who was breaking the law. As such, prosecuting violators was a possible task.

Not so with digital media. Anyone with a multimedia computer and an Internet account can go out on the World Wide Web and gather logos, pictures, music, videos, software programs, articles, and anything else of value to the original creator. Then they can take this material and rearrange it any way they want. Want to put a dress on Michael Jackson? No problem. Want to make Mel Torme sing songs by Nirvana? Easy. And most importantly, the digital pirate can broadcast these mutations over the Internet by e-mail, or post them to a Web site. As you can see, it's almost impossible to control this black market in digital content. In cases of large infractions — by your competitors, for example — you might be able to take legal action and win, but it's not feasible to round up every petty miscreant on the Internet.

As a digital marketer, you need to accept the fact that, in all but the largest cases, you don't have a viable way to stop infractions, or seek damages. Because of this reality, consider making your trademark digital content freely available to the world. Create a section on your Web site that deals with the issue. Instead of prosecuting people, use the exchange of digital trademark material to develop closer relationships with your customers. Invite them to download your logo and place it on their Web site. After all, having your logo on computers all over the world might be a good thing.

DIGITAL LEGAL LIABILITIES

Before you venture into the cybermarket, you need to understand the legal liabilities of digital marketing. In addition to the laws which exist in the traditional world, there are a number of legal peculiarities which pertain to digital and online technology.

Copyright and trademark infringement: While you can attempt to protect yourself against copyright and trademark infractions against you, you must also guard against exposing yourself to legal prosecution from others. Don't use logos, graphics, pictures, text, or software from other traditional or digital sources, unless you receive permission from their creators. If you receive digital content from someone, find out where they got it from. If they didn't produce it themselves, make sure to get permission from the original creator.

Here is some additional information about copyright and trademarks.

- All original creations, such as articles, photographs, movies, and graphic art are copyright protected.
- No notice is required to establish a copyright.
- Every e-mail you distribute and receive is copyright.
- You cannot reproduce or distribute copyright material, even if you don't charge for it.
- Information in newsgroups and Web sites is copyright.
- You can use a portion of an article or book, but it must be short and attributed to the originator (as in the quotes preceding each chapter in this book).
- Under normal conditions, names and titles can't be copyrighted. However, names can be trademarked if you use them to refer to your product. For example, the word "Newton" is trademarked by Apple Computers to use for its personal digital assistant, but there is nothing stopping someone from trademarking the word "Newton" to sell toasters. However, you cannot use a trademarked name if your use will undermine the image of the other company's product or service.

Digital fraud: As is the case in the traditional marketing environment, you cannot make false or misleading advertising claims on the Internet, or by using any other digital marketing tools. Recently, the US Federal Trade Commission charged nine companies with digital fraud. The companies posted Web sites which advertised spurious promises such as "Guaranteed Credit Repair" and "Our Home Workers Earned an Average Income of $38,000 a Year." Eight of the cases were settled out of court, and one was settled in federal district court. So watch yourself. Law enforcement agencies are starting to take seriously unlawful digital marketing practises.

Digital contests: In Canada, promotional contests are governed by the Criminal Code and the Competitions Act. The rules of running a contest on the Internet or through any other digital tool are:

- You cannot give prizes away using games of chance which require the entrant to pay in order to participate.
- If participants don't have to make a purchase to enter a contest, they must answer a skill testing question to receive the prize if they win.
- You must make public the number of prizes, the value of the prizes, and the chances of winning (if you know them).
- If you make a contest available to people outside Canada, you must meet all the Canadian rules and regulations.
- If someone outside Canada offers a contest to Canadians, the contest must meet all the Canadian rules and regulations.
- If you run a contest on the Internet, make sure to consult a lawyer who specializes in marketing law.

Online provider liability: If you set up a BBS or a Web site, you are responsible for all the content seen on it, or transmitted through it. For example, if you set up a private online network (BBS), you are responsible for all the content exchanged on the system, even if you have no knowledge of it. If someone decides to use your BBS to distribute pornography or hate literature, you could be arrested. If you set up a Web site Chat Room, and people use it to conduct criminal activity, you could be found guilty as an accomplice. If you set up a newsgroup, and people use it to slam your competitors, you could be sued for libel or slander. Although punishing the online service provider for the crimes of its users seems unfair, there are many precedents of this happening.

Recently, the Church of Scientology sued an Internet service provider for giving its subscribers access to a newsgroup which criticizes the church. A lower court in the United States ruled that the church has a possible case against the ISP, even though the newsgroup is available through every other Internet provider in the world. Taken to an absurd degree, this type of liability is chilling. What happens if you provide links on your Web site which lead to a Web site that has further links to hate literature? Are you promoting hate literature? Are you engaging in a criminal activity? Because every site on the Internet eventually leads to every other site, what legal responsibility do you assume when you set up a Web site? Unfortunately, no one really knows the answer to these questions because the laws are too ambiguous.

As time goes by and the international legal system begins to grapple with these issues, some of these laws may be rescinded. But until then, you must make sure your online network, or any other digital tool, is not used by your customers or prospects to conduct an illegal or unethical activity. Remember, you could be legally culpable even if you have no knowledge of the activity.

KEEPING SECRETS IN THE DIGITAL AGE

Data security and encryption: Data security is one of the central issues of digital marketing. Because the Internet is a public highway, the information which travels through it can be picked up and read by anyone who has the knowledge and capability to do so. If security measures have not been taken to scramble the data, or code it, the information is totally unsecured. In many cases, people don't care about data security. When you send an e-mail message to a friend, you usually don't care if someone intercepts it. It's no different than someone at the post office opening up your letter, or someone listening to your conversation on a cellular telephone scanner. You take that risk. But when you want to send a confidential e-mail to someone in your company, or give someone your credit card number on the Internet, it's a different matter. You want to send a secret message which only the recipient can unravel and read. That's where data encryption comes in.

Data encryption has been used for centuries to scramble and descramble messages. The people who develop encrypted messages are called ciphers or cryptographers, and their craft is called cryptography. Until a short time ago, cryptography was based on a "single key" model. The key was used to scramble and descramble the message. As long as the sender and recipient had the key, they could send each other cryptic messages without worrying that they would be intercepted and deciphered by others. The problem was distributing the key. If someone got hold of the key, the whole scheme fell apart.

In 1977, a new method of cryptography called Public Key Cryptography was invented by Whitfield Diffie and Martin Hellman. In this model, there are two keys — a Public Key (encryption key) and a Private Key (decryption key). The recipient creates both keys and makes the Public Key available to everyone. Then anyone can send him or her a private code message (using the Public Key), but only the recipient can unscramble it (using the Private Key.)

Through the use of Public Key encryption, it is possible to send and receive private messages over the Internet and other online networks. It is also possible to verify the identity of the sender, and the identity of the recipient, which is a necessary precondition for the viable use of credit cards over the Internet.

Unfortunately, the development of data encryption standards for the Internet has been hampered by infighting among competing encryption inventors. As well, the field of digital cryptography has been broadsided by the US federal laws which restrict the export of encryption technology to certain countries. Similar to book readers in *Fahrenheit 451*, digital cryptographers have been singled out for harassment by government authorities. Phil Zimmermann, the inventor of an e-mail encryption software program called Pretty Good Privacy (PGP), was investigated for three years by the US government before the threat of prosecution was dropped last January. Authorities are worried that an unbreakable encryption standard will make it impossible for them to read e-mail sent on the Internet by criminals and law-abiding citizens alike.

Internet fire walls: If you have a network-wide Internet connection, you need to use a fire wall to restrict access to your network from unwanted visitors on the Internet. A fire wall is essential because this kind of connection exposes the data on your network to anyone on the Internet who has the savvy to break in. Using the fire wall, you can make your network accessible to welcome parties, and keep everyone else out. And like a one-way filter, the fire wall will let you go out to the Internet, but won't let people come in, unless you want them to.

Encrypted data tunnels: If your company has a number of offices across the country, or around the world, all the digital data you send from office to office over the Internet may be opened and read by other parties. To secure the privacy of this data, you can rent leased lines instead of using the Internet, or set up an Encrypted Data Tunnel. The tunnel encrypts your data to make it unreadable to anyone who intercepts it. Note: The Internet is considered an appropriate way to send noncritical data from one office to another within an organization. For mission-critical applications — such as point-of-sale credit card authorizations — the Internet is considered too slow, unreliable, and insecure. For these applications, leased lines are preferred to the Internet.

ELECTRONIC MONEY AND ONLINE TRANSACTIONS

The development of a secure and verifiable form of electronic money will be the catalyst for an explosion in the field of digital marketing. Also known as cybercash or digital cash, e-money will become the standard currency of the digital age. You'll be able to load e-money onto smart cards using readers attached to your telephone, or download it from your bank account to your hard drive. You'll use it to buy products and services online, and transfer it to your friends and relatives. You'll also carry around a digital purse with electronic money in it, and use it like you use cash today.

Daunting hurdles must be overcome before digital money becomes a reality, and many questions remain unanswered. Should electronic money be based on existing national currencies, or should a new international electronic currency be created? How can you verify if the electronic money is real or counterfeit? If someone figures out how to duplicate digital money, would there be a financial crisis? How can you encrypt the transmission of electronic money to preserve the privacy of the buyers and sellers?

These question are just the beginning. The issue of privacy becomes a potential nightmare in a world of digital money. When every transaction you make is digital, it is possible to track everything you do. If you use a smart card to buy a coke or pay for a parking meter, the machine can figure out who you are. Big Brother won't need a television camera to keep track of you; he will simply follow you from one vending machine to another.

Secure online transactions: Until digital money becomes widespread, digital marketers will have to convince customers to use credit cards to buy products and services online. What is needed is an encryption standard which enables the private transmission of credit card information over the Internet. Unfortunately, a number of different companies are competing to establish the standard, and the competition will cause confusion in the marketplace. For example, a company called CyberCash Inc. has introduced a utility called Cybercash Wallet. You use the wallet on your computer to store your VISA, MasterCard, American Express, and Discovery card numbers. All the data is protected by passwords and transmitted in an encrypted format. When you want to make a purchase, you send the merchant the information from your CyberCash wallet. Another group has developed an electronic payment protocol called Paypro, which also facilitates online shopping and banking. Unfortunately, the emergence of multiple transaction formats will be their undoing. Unless a standard is developed, and every online shopper uses it, there will be too many different payment systems, and the consumer will tire of sorting through all of them. This confusion will seriously undermine the viability of online shopping.

TAKE THE DIGITAL HIGH ROAD

As digital and online technology becomes an integral part of our lives, these issues and many more will have to be dealt with. The role of national governments will be called into question. Our entire social order could change in unexpected ways. We could become prisoners of digital technology, or we could be liberated by it.

It's your responsibility to understand these issues and contribute to the debate. As an active user of digital technology, you are in an ideal position to assess its impact and influence on our society. As you use this technology to make money and achieve your business objectives, I challenge you to take the high road so that the digital age becomes known as the second Age of Enlightenment, rather than the second Dark Ages.

Now I invite you to read the final section, The Future of Digital Marketing, which looks at what it might be like to be a marketer in the future, both near and far.

SECTION FIVE

THE FUTURE OF DIGITAL MARKETING

CHAPTER 16

BEYOND TECHNOPIA

The Dimensional Age, which has replaced the Age of Nanotechnology, is a time of great change and turmoil. With the discovery of the Dimensional Corridor, consumers and marketers alike are grappling with many issues, especially the issues of cross-dimensional trade, corridor overload, and molecular encryption.

Strategic Marketing for the Dimensional Age
Bill Bishop, XXVII, 2525

As time goes by, you will find some things never change... I think these three possible futures will illustrate my point:

THE DIGITAL BOOM YEARS (2020)

Through his virtual reality contact lenses, Milford McLuhan sees that another 150 thousand digital dollars have been uploaded to his bank account by Malagasy Incorporated, a software company. For the ninth time in three days, Malagasy has purchased data from Milford's online warehouse to use in the design of underwater mining software.

Scanning through his holomailbox, Milford activates a message from Evelyn Jung, the owner of Malagasy. "Good morning, Milford," she says, looking very pleased. "As you can see, I downloaded another 500 tetrabytes last night. Your data is error free and beautifully designed. My compiling robots have been working nonstop for two days now and the project is almost done. We just need you to get us another 800 tetrabytes from the GlobeNet resource bank by the end of the day. Can you do it?"

Milford thinks about it for a minute while gazing seaward from his yacht moored off Tortola in the British Virgin Islands. He has been thinking about scuba diving this morning, but decides to take the contract. He sends Jung a holomessage saying the data will be compiled before noon.

Jacking into the holographic GlobeNet, Milford can see that data trading is active. More than 250 trillion tetrabytes of data have been traded on the CyberMarket in the last two hours. Concerned that prices are rising, Milford speaks to his data agent, the amiable Mr. Blue.

"What's the opening fix on encrypted biodata?" Milford asks. "Can I put an offer in at $50,000 for 800 tetrabytes?"

Mr. Blue scans the RFP data listings and comes back with the available offerings. "There are 1,000 tetrabytes of raw biodata for sale from an Asian syndicate, but they're asking $90,000 firm."

Milford doesn't like to buy raw biodata if it isn't encrypted, but he is in a hurry. "Have it uploaded immediately into my San Francisco synthetic data processor, and withdraw the funds from my Swiss e-money account."

Within minutes, the data has arrived, and Milford sets about processing it. He calls up his three-dimensional media artist and asks her to design the data architecture, and sends a message to his data cryptographer asking him to compile a private security code sequence.

As he prepares breakfast in the galley, Milford can see that the data is being assembled in record time. The new DNA processors are running at lightning speed, calculating more than 50 trillion instructions per millisecond. By the time Milford has finished his roast beef sandwich, the project is done and ready for the client.

"That's enough work for today," Milford thinks to himself, as he turns off his GlobeNet connection. "I think I'll do some scuba diving after all."

THE DAWN OF THE BIOLOGICAL ECONOMY (2096)

As the world approaches the 22nd century, the Digital Economy is being usurped by the Biological Economy. Many digital workers are being laid off, but new jobs are being created in the biological sector. Every day more than 100 million people exchange their genes on the Bioreticulum.

For some people, the Biological Economy is a curse. The leaders of the global government, operating on the outmoded paradigms of the Digital Age, are not equipped to deal with the rapid upheavals being fostered by bioengineering technology. Legislation has been tabled to restrict the use of biological technology and to require the registration of all gene pools. Digital unions, which formed on the defunct Internet at the beginning of the century, are clogging GlobeNet router points to protest the loss of digital benefits and online job security.

For other people, the Biological Economy is a blessing. Young people, who never understood all the excitement about digital technology, are lining up to take biological courses on the GlobeNet. The 12-year-old girl who developed a brain gene-splicing technique earned more than 50 trillion dollars when her initial public offering sold out in 30 seconds on the CyberMarket.

For marketers, the Biological Economy presents many challenges. Educated on the Strategic Digital Marketing Model, veteran marketers are finding that the old rules don't work anymore. Digital marketing tools such as smart cards and online networks have lost their appeal to consumers who spend their waking hours searching for new gene stations. Visits on GlobeNet BBS sites have been falling steadily as more and more people meet and exchange cell plasma on the Bioreticulum.

What is needed is a Strategic Biological Marketing Model. Under this model, consumers are attracted to your Biological Domain because you provide them with unique gene material, gene enzymes, and plasmid vectors. When they access you through your biological tools — such as DNA strands or molecular inhibitors — make sure you record their chromosomes in your biobase. You can use this biodata to create unique bioproducts and biopromotions.

One possible strategy is to develop your own proprietary Biological Bulletin Board (BBB) which runs on the Bioreticulum. Take a proactive approach and hook up each of your best clients to the BBB using customized cellular connection equipment. Give them direct access to your private biodata, and set up private conferences such as "Cytoplasmic Chromosomes" or "Mitochondria Mating." By giving your customers access to these restricted biological resources, you foster closer relationships with them.

Ultimately, digital companies must adapt to survive in the future. They must takes steps now to "biologicalize" their business. Learn about the basics of movable genetic elements and eugenic upgrading. Get on the Bioreticulum and find out what your competitors are up to. But don't just post static recombinant DNA molecules on the Bioreticulum. Study the Strategic Biological Marketing Model!

THE YEAR OF THE JOY DIMENSION (2525)

In the year 2525, the Dimensional Corridor is discovered by a five-year-old boy playing in his father's closet. At first, no one believes his tale about the Joy Dimension, until a curious news reporter investigates the story, and reports it is true. And what a story it is. The Joy Dimension is a paradise where every dream comes true, and the story never ends.

The discovery of the Joy Dimension is a mixed blessing for the world. At the time, the Nano Economy is in full bloom. Using microscopic nanorobots, life forms are able to take molecules apart and put the atoms back together into any type of new molecule.

(For example, you can take a landfill site full of garbage and turn it into a school or a lakeside resort.) Nanotechnology gives sentient beings the power to build anything from any material. Unfortunately, dimensional jumping — as it is known — brings an end to the Nano Economy. No one is interested anymore in building things to make their lives better when they can simply jump over to the Joy Dimension. Within months of its discovery, dimensional jumping causes the collapse of almost every nanocompany on the face of the earth.

Fortunately, a few intrepid entrepreneurs survive the upheaval by "dimensionalizing" their business. They look at the dimensional marketing environment and see great opportunity. They realize there is more to the Dimensional Age than just the Joy Dimension. They go out and discover dozens of other dimensions such as the Soulful Dimension, the Rhapsodic Dimension, and the Dimension of Eternal Calm. They set up marketing kiosks on the Dimensional Corridor to encourage people to take an alternative jump rather than always going to the Joy Dimension.

As the popularity of dimension jumping grows, many problems and issues are raised. Is the corridor only for humans? Should life forms be able to use the corridor for free? And most importantly, who controls the corridor? Should anyone be allowed to set up a corridor portal, or should it be regulated and restricted to a few large corridor utilities?

As a marketer in the Dimensional Age, your task is to create new and exciting dimensional experiences. Get to know your customers. Ask them: "What dimensions do you visit most often? What kinds of dimensions do you want to experience?" Put together innovative dimensional packages tailored to each individual person.

And above all, remember your customer is the most important part of your marketing program. No matter what technology you are using — digital, biological, nano, or dimensional — the customer is *always* right.

GLOSSARY OF TERMS

Analog: Information stored or measured as an electronic voltage is known as analog. Television, radio, VCRs, and rotary telephones use an analog method to store and transmit information.

Bandwidth: Bandwidth measures the capacity of a transmission medium such as twisted pair telephone lines, coaxial cables, or fiber-optic cables. The greater the number of bytes which can be transmitted at a time, the greater the bandwidth. The use of elaborate graphics, digital video, and multimedia for promotional purposes on the Internet is severely constrained by the lack of sufficient bandwidth.

Baud rate: This is the rate at which digital information is transmitted and received by a modem. Baud rate is measured in bits per second (bps). Typical modems come in speeds of 14,400 (14.4 kbps) and 28,800 (28.8 kbps) bits per second. The use of cable modems promises baud rates of more than 500,000 bps.

BBS (Bulletin Board Service or System): A BBS is a digital meeting place where people can exchange information over telephone lines or over the Internet. Subscribers to a BBS can post e-mail messages or digital files to online conferences, and read or download files from other subscribers. You can create your own BBS system and use it to connect your customers to your company's computer network.

Bit: A bit is a single binary digit, either 1 or 0.

Byte: A string of eight bits (such as 10101101) is known as a byte. One thousand (1,000) bytes is equal to one kilobyte. One million (1,000,000) is equal to a megabyte.

Calling card: Also known as a prepaid or long-distance calling card. The holder of the card calls a 1-800 number, enters a PIN number, and makes long-distance calls based on the face value of the card (such as $5, $10, and $20). Promotional messages can be incorporated into the interactive voice-response messages heard by the caller. (Large carriers such as Bell Canada issue calling cards to their customers. These cards have a magnetic strip and a PIN number and long-distance fees are charged directly to your Bell account.)

CD-ROM: Stands for Compact Disk Read-Only Memory. It looks likes an audio compact disk and holds 640 megabytes of digital information, and is used for storing multimedia presentations and large amounts of information. To use a CD-ROM, you need a CD-ROM drive on your computer. You can produce a multimedia promotion and distribute it on CD-ROM.

Cellular radio: You can create a promotional newscast and broadcast it over the cellular telephone system. Cellular telephone users will access the broadcast by dialing a number such as *88. They will not be charged for the call. It requires making arrangements with cellular telephone companies. Costs can be offset by selling advertising to other companies.

Chat room: Many Web sites have chat rooms where you converse electronically with other Internet users. As bandwidth increases, chat rooms will incorporate live video-conferencing and virtual reality. You can set up a chat room as a promotional tool to attract people to your Web site. It is a novelty item at this point.

Commercial online services: These are large bulletin board systems which provide their own content in addition to access to the Internet. Subscribers pay a monthly fee for basic services, and a per-minute charge for specialized information. The biggest services are Prodigy, America Online, CompuServe, and The Microsoft Network. You can reach the subscribers of a commercial online service by sponsoring a discussion group or by setting up an online store. With the advent of the World Wide Web, the closed nature of these services calls into question their marketing potential.

Customer database: This is a database which contains information about your customers and prospects. It can be simple, such as a mailing list, or it can be complex with extensive data on each customer.

Custom Internet platform: This is a private online system, developed for a specific purpose, which runs on the Internet. For example, you can create a unique ordering system for your store which runs over the Internet. The point is, you don't need to limit yourself to the World Wide Web or other standard Internet platforms such as File Transfer Protocol (FTP). You can create your own.

Databases: Like a digital filing cabinet, you use a customer database to store the names, street addresses, and telephone/fax/e-mail addresses of your customers, along with a profile of their preferences, needs, buying patterns, and credit history. A customer database is the primary digital tool of the Strategic Digital Marketing Model.

Digital: Information stored in the form of 1s and 0s is known as digital. All information stored and processed by computer, including text, sound, graphics, and video, is digital in composition. The opposite of digital is analog.

Digital assets: These are assets your company has in a digital form. This includes database information, intellectual property, transactional data, multimedia content, and any other digital information that can be sold or rented to another party.

Digital cheques: Digital cheques contain a magnetic strip or bar code. You can issue them instead of coupons for redemption at retail stores. To redeem the digital cheque, the customer fills out a survey on the back and presents it to the retailer. The cheque is deposited by the retailer and returned to you within days through the banking system. The survey answers are scanned or manually entered into your customer database.

Digital communications audit: You conduct a digital communications audit to determine the technical capabilities and preferences of your customers and prospects. For example, you can conduct a survey to find out if your customers use the World Wide Web or if they use CD-ROMs.

Digital Domain: This is the digital and online environment your customers and prospects enter to learn about your company and its products and services. Your Digital Domain is reached through digital tools such as the Internet, BBS, interactive voice-response, and fax-on-demand systems.

Digital intermediary: This is a person or organization controlling the flow of digital information for an entire industry. For example, a car dealer can set up an online service that lists automobiles for sale by every car manufacturer, not just their own cars. As the digital intermediary, they earn a commission on every car sold in the entire industry.

Digital marketing: The use of digital technology and processes in the development, distribution, and promotion of products and services.

Digital privacy intermediaries (DPI): These are digital devices — such as anonymous e-mail, voice mail, and fax mailboxes — used to protect the personal privacy of individuals.

Digital Videodisk (DVD): This is a new type of CD-ROM with significantly more storage capacity than current CD-ROMs. Within a few years, you will be able to distribute elaborate multimedia promotions on DVD.

Domain name: A domain name is your company's address on the Internet. A typical domain name is biginc.com or biginc.on.ca. If you do not have a domain name registered, I suggest you do so immediately. If you wait, another company may take the one you want.

Electronic forms: Electronic forms are filled out on computer rather than on paper. You can send electronic order forms to your customers on disk or through e-mail. When the forms are returned to you, the data can be downloaded directly into your customer database.

E-mail: Stands for electronic mail. You can send and receive e-mail messages over the Internet or internally over private networks. Because e-mail is intrusive, it is one of the most powerful digital marketing tools.

E-money: An electronic currency used to purchase products and services over the Internet. It is also known as cybercash.

Encryption: Methods used to secure the transmission of digital information over the Internet and over other digital media. Involves the use of complex mathematical formulas.

Encrypted data tunnel: An encrypted data tunnel secures data sent over the Internet between offices in the same company. The tunnel encrypts the data to make it unreadable to anyone who intercepts it.

Fax mailbox: A fax mailbox is used to store faxes until they are retrieved by the owner of the box. To retrieve faxes, you dial a telephone number, enter a password, and indicate which fax machine you wish to have your faxes sent to. You can set up a private fax mailbox for your customers and provide them with individualized information.

Fax-on-demand: With a fax-on-demand system, you can provide customized fax information automatically upon request. To get documents, you dial up the system, and enter your fax number and a code for each of the documents you desire. The documents are automatically sent within minutes to your fax machine.

Fire wall: If you have a network-wide Internet connection, you need to use a device called a fire wall to restrict access to your network from unwanted visitors on the Internet. A fire wall is essential because a network-wide connection exposes the data on your network to anyone on the Internet who has the savvy to break in.

FTP (File Transfer Protocol): You use FTP software to transfer digital files from one computer to another over the Internet.

Flatline database: A flatline database is the opposite of a relational database. Each flatline database file is a separate entity. Information cannot be shared between different database files as is the case with a relational database.

HTML: Stands for Hyper Text Markup Language. This is the programming language used to create content for the World Wide Web.

Ident-a-call: A digital technology used to identify the number and origin of an incoming telephone call.

Industry-wide information system: This is an online service used to control the flow of information within an industry. The person or organization that runs an industry-wide information system is called a digital intermediary.

Interactive kiosk: An interactive kiosk is used to give customers a way to browse through information on a computer. You can set up an inexpensive interactive kiosk in your store by running an internal Web site on a stand-alone PC.

Interactive survey: This is a survey completed using a digital tool such as a Web site, voice mail system, BBS, or an interactive kiosk. The results of an interactive survey are fed directly into your customer database.

Interactive television: Your television will become a two-way digital tool that will allow you to select options using a handheld channel changer. The advent of interactive television will open up a vast new audience for digital marketers.

Internet: The Internet is a global online network of computer networks.

Internet service provider (ISP): An ISP is a company that provides access to the Internet for companies and individuals.

IVR (interactive voice response): IVR allows you to access and select from a menu of audio information using the keys on your Touch-Tone telephone. Because everyone uses a telephone, IVR is one of the most powerful digital marketing tools.

Intranet: An Intranet is an internal communications system based on the World Wide Web platform. Intranets have become popular because they are easy to set up and maintain and can be accessed by many different kinds of computer platforms. Unlike the Internet, an Intranet is only accessible to people within an organization.

IP address: An IP Address is your numeric address on the Internet (i.e., 121.154.6.44.).

Latent digital capabilities: These are digital capabilities and information resources in your organization which are not being utilized to their fullest potential.

Loyalty card programs: These are programs set up by a company to reward its best customers and to encourage repeat business. Members of a loyalty program usually receive points or other rewards by presenting a plastic card when making a purchase.

Mail list server: A mail list server is used to distribute e-mail messages to a group of people on the Internet. To join a mailing list about a particular subject (e.g., bonsai tree pruning), you send an e-mail message to the mail list server. You can set up an Internet mailing list to send out information to your customers and prospects.

Market segment: A market segment is a part of your total market defined by particular common characteristics. You divide your customers and prospects into different segments to identify their unique needs and preferences.

Marketing myopia: A term coined by Theodore Levitt to describe the condition in which a company loses sight of its real business or mandate. For example, a bank isn't only in the banking business; it's in the financial services business.

Marketing technopia: A term I coined to describe the condition in which a company becomes obsessed with technology to the point of forgetting its customers and its real business objectives.

Modem: Stands for modulator/demodular. A device used to send and receive digital information from one computer to another over telephone lines.

Multimedia: Refers to the use of text, graphics, audio and video to present digital information.

Network-wide Internet connection: Also known as a full Internet connection, it refers to a network of computers connected continuously to the Internet over high-speed data lines.

Newsgroups: These are discussion groups on the Internet which cover a particular subject. There were more than 22,000 newsgroups on the Internet as of early 1998.

Online services: These are information and function-related services accessed using a modem and a computer. The Internet, BBSs, and commercial services, such as America Online and CompuServe, are examples of online services.

Online shopping: This refers to the purchase of products and services using online services such as the World Wide Web.

Online shopping malls: These are World Wide Web sites that feature a number of different stores offering a wide range of products and services.

Pay phone services: These services pay people to listen to promotional messages over the telephone, similar to a reverse 1-900 number.

Personal digital assistant (PDA): These are small handheld computers that allow you to send and receive e-mail and fax messages over wireless or cellular transmission systems.

Personal identification number (PIN): This is a series of numbers or letters that serve to identify a person as the rightful owner of a transaction medium such as a banking or smart card.

Private online network: This is an online network accessible only to people who have a user ID and a password. To use it as a marketing tool, you can set up a private online network for your customers. It is also known as a BBS.

Privacy agent: In the near future, privacy agents will be used to protect the privacy of individuals. If a marketer wants information about a person, he will approach his privacy agent and negotiate a price for data.

Privacy ombudsman: This is an individual appointed in a company or organization to champion the privacy rights of customers. For example, a privacy ombudsman makes sure customer data is not used in an unethical manner.

RAM (random access memory): This is the live, active memory of your computer measured in megabytes. Most new computers run on at least 8 megabytes of RAM.

Relational database: This is a database format which allows information in different database files to be shared with each other. When you set up a customer database, use a relational database program.

Request for Proposal (RFP) robots: These are future devices and processes which will allow you to make your consumer needs known to marketers while maintaining your anonymity.

Reverse 1-900: When you dial up a reverse 1-900 number, you receive a credit on your telephone bill. It can be used by marketers to get people to listen to promotional messages.

Router: This is a piece of equipment that controls the flow of digital information on the Internet.

Screen saver: A screen saver is used to protect the quality of a computer monitor. If a computer is left idle for a certain length of time, the screen saver displays a picture or moving graphical image. You can create a screen saver as a promotional item and distribute it on the Internet.

Search engine: Search engines are used on the Internet to find Web sites. They are also used to find information in a database.

Smart cards: These are cards which can receive, store, and transmit digital information such as electronic money or medical records.

Strategic Digital Marketing Model: A model I have developed to guide you in the development of marketing programs using digital and online technology.

TCP/IP (transmission control protocol/Internet protocol): All information transmitted over the Internet must be formatted based on the TCP/IP standard. You can create your own Internet platform as long as it adheres to TCP/IP.

Universal resource locator (URL): This is the address of your Web site on the Internet. A typical URL is http://www.biginc.on.ca.

Video-mail: This is the next generation of e-mail. Digital video images are captured using a digital camera and sent as an attachment to an e-mail message. The recipient can open up the message and view the video. It won't become practical until greater bandwidth is generally available.

Virtual reality (VR): This is the use of sophisticated hardware and software to simulate a "virtual" environment. Although the commercial applications of VR are limited and expensive at this time, it will become more viable as computers become more powerful in the next ten years.

Web server: This is the computer that holds your home page and other documents on the World Wide Web. It is connected directly to the Internet and is accessed using a browser software such as Netscape Navigator or Mosaic.

Web site: This refers to your content on the World Wide Web. A Web site is located on a computer connected directly to the Internet.

World Wide Web: This is the most commercial platform on the Internet. It allows users to jump from one computer to another on the Internet in order to view pages with text, graphics, and other multimedia features.

SUGGESTED READING

Beck, Nuala. *Excelerate: Growing In The New Economy*. Toronto: HarperCollins, 1995.

Davis, Stan and Bill Davidson. *2020 Vision*. New York: Simon & Schuster, 1991.

Gilder, George. *Microcosm*. New York: Simon & Schuster, 1989.

Hughes, Arthur M. *The Complete Database Marketer*. Toronto: Irwin Professional Publishing, 1996.

Negroponte, Nicholas P. *being digital*. New York: Knopf, 1995.

Penzias A. *Ideas and Information: Managing in a High-Tech World*. New York: W.W. Norton & Co., 1989.

Peppers, Don and Martha Rogers, Ph.D. *The One to One Future*. New York: Doubleday, 1993.

Postman, Neil. *Technopoly*. New York: Vintage Books, 1993.

Rapp, Stan and Tom Collins. *MaxiMarketing*. New York: McGraw-Hill, 1989.

Sullivan, Dan. *The Great Crossover*. Toronto: The Strategic Coach, 1994.

Tapscott, Don. *The Digital Economy*. Toronto: McGraw-Hill, 1996.

Toffler, Alvin. *The Third Wave*. New York: Bantam, 1980.

Science Fiction Books

Asimov, Issac. *Foundation and Empire*. New York: Ballantine Books, 1952.

Asimov, Isaac. *The Gods Themselves*. Doubleday, 1972.

Asimov, Isaac. *I, Robot*. New York: Doubleday, 1960.

Bradbury, Ray. *Fahrenheit 451*. New York: Ballantine Books, 1953.

Clarke, Arthur C. *2001 A Space Odyssey*. London: Penguin Books, 1968.

Dick, Philip K. *Do Androids Dream of Electric Sheep?* New York: Ballantine Books, 1968.

Heinlein, Robert A. *Stranger In A Strange Land*. New York: Berkley Medallion Books, 1968.

Herbert, Frank. *Dune*. New York: Berkley Medallion Books, 1965.

Huxley, Aldous. *Brave New World*. London: Penguin Books Ltd., 1967.

Orwell, George. *Nineteen Eighty-Four*. London: Penguin Books, 1949.

Pohl, Frederik and C.M. Kornbluth. *The Space Merchants*. New York: Ballantine Books, 1952.

Vonnegut, Kurt. *The Sirens of Titan*. New York: Dell Publishing, 1988.

Wells, H.G. *The Time Machine*. New York: Penguin, 1984.

Digital Media

Clute, John and Peter Nicholls. *The Multimedia Encyclopedia of Science Fiction*. Toronto: Grolier Incorporated, 1995.

The Grolier Multimedia Encyclopedia. Toronto: Grolier Incorporated, 1995.

Reference

Boone, Louis E., David L. Kurtz and M. Dale Beckman. *Foundations of Marketing*. Toronto: Holt, Rinehard and Winston of Canada, 1982.

Elliot, Joe and Tim Worsley, Eds. *Multimedia: The Complete Guide*. Toronto: élan press, 1996.